Championship

DATE DUE		

**507
BAR**

**3 24571 0900168 9
Bardhan-Quallen,
Sudipta.**

**Championship science
fair projects : 100
sure-to-win
experiments**

Championship
Science Fair
PROJECTS

100 Sure-to-Win Experiments

Sudipta Bardhan-Quallen

STERLING

New York / London
www.sterlingpublishing.com/kids

STERLING and the distinctive Sterling logo are registered trademarks of
Sterling Publishing Co., Inc.

Library of Congress Cataloging-in-Publication Data Available

10   9   8   7   6   5   4   3   2

Published in 2004 by Sterling Publishing Co., Inc.
387 Park Avenue South
New York, NY 10016
Copyright © 2004 by Sudipta Bardhan-Quallen
Illustrations Copyright © 2004 by Rob Collinet
Distributed in Canada by Sterling Publishing
^{c}/o Canadian Manda Group, 165 Dufferin Street
Toronto, Ontario, Canada M6K 3H6
Distributed in the United Kingdom by GMC Distribution Services,
Castle Place, 166 High Street, Lewes, East Sussex, England BN7 1XU
Distributed in Australia by Capricorn Link (Australia) Pty Ltd.
P.O. Box 704, Windsor, NSW 2756, Australia

Printed in China
All Rights Reserved

Sterling   ISBN 13: 978-1-4027-1138-1 Hardcover
ISBN 10: 1-4027-1138-7
ISBN 13: 978-1-4027-4838-7 Paperback
ISBN 10: 1-4027-4838-8

For information about custom editions, special sales, premium and
corporate purchases, please contact Sterling Special Sales
Department at 800-805-5489 or specialsales@sterlingpub.com

Contents

Introduction

Your Project

Designing a project for a science fair may seem complicated, intimidating, or even boring, but it doesn't have to be any of those things. Science experiments can be a lot of fun, as long as you approach them correctly. This book is designed to help you with the planning process. The 100 projects outlined here give detailed, step-by-step instructions for projects that have been proven to work. These projects were developed to answer specific questions from various areas of science. Whatever your interests or skill level, there are several experiments in this book that will fit your needs.

Successful science fair projects are most often those that focus less on following a set of instructions and more on figuring out some problem in science. For example, if you are interested in learning about how plants grow, you could ask, "Do plants always grow toward sunlight?" or "How does gravity affect a plant's roots?" If, on the other hand, you are interested in magnetism, you could ask, "How does a magnet's shape affect the magnetic field it creates?" or "Can magnetic fields generate electricity?" After you've defined the question, you structure an experiment that answers the question, and research any background information relevant to the experiment. Understanding the background information will help you generate a *hypothesis*, which is the predicted outcome of the experiment—the answer to your question. A main goal of the experiment is proving or disproving the hypothesis.

Whenever you perform an experiment, it is important that you take careful notes recording your observations. All of the projects in this book include an outline of the results you should see if everything progresses properly. Don't be discouraged if your results are different from what you expected! Believe it or not, even professional scientists often run into a situation where two people come up with different results. First, try focusing on repeating the experiment to see if your results change. If you've tried a few times and still don't see the predicted results, try to figure out why your results are different. For example, if you try the "Push an Egg into a Bottle" experiment and the egg will not go in, check to see if the mouth of the bottle is too narrow or if there are small chips in the rim of the bottle preventing the formation of a good air seal. The goal of any science experiment is to learn, and you can learn just as much from something that seems unsuccessful as you can from an experiment that runs smoothly.

Keep your mind open as you do the projects in this book. If you come up with a question that the experiment does not answer, think about how you could design an extension to the project or even a new experiment to answer it. Many of the projects in the book already come with suggestions for ways to extend the experiment. Use the book as a foundation for your own scientific curiosity. In fact, if you find a way to redesign a project that is especially interesting, tell us about it!

Materials

The experiments in this book have been designed to use mostly inexpensive items found around the house or in a supermarket. On occasion, a special material might be necessary, and the project instructions will tell you where you are likely to find the items. Read through the chapters before you select which experiments you will do—often, you will find that a specialty item will be useful in more than one project.

A Word about Safety

All of the experiments in this book have been tested for safety, but you should still take the proper precautions to ensure that no one or nothing gets hurt in any way. The first thing you must do is read the directions completely before you start a project. Make sure you understand all the steps and that you've gathered all the

proper materials. If an experiment calls for using the stove or oven, it is a good idea to have an adult help you. This also holds true when you use certain chemicals like rubbing alcohol, bleach, acetone, ammonia, or methyl salicylate. The projects requiring adult help are clearly marked with safety warnings so you'll know when to ask for supervision.

Some of the experiments involve the use of animals, like earthworms or goldfish. It is very important that you treat the animals respectfully and do your best to avoid hurting them. Humane treatment of animal subjects is very important in science; even in those cases where a lab animal is sacrificed during an experiment, scientists follow very specific rules to prevent the animal from experiencing unnecessary pain or discomfort.

Collecting Data

The projects in this book range from building batteries to growing grafted plants to exploring how earthworms learn. The way you document your results will vary as much as the experiments themselves.

The most important thing you can do is write everything down—what kind and amounts of materials you used, the temperature and lighting conditions in the room you worked in, who helped you with any of the steps—in addition to the results you see. Your written records will be most helpful in writing your science report and figuring out why a project did or did not work as expected.

In addition to written records, you should document your experiments in as many ways as you can. Sometimes you will be able to keep your whole project for display. Other times, it will be best to take photographs or video. Make sketches when you can, and find interesting ways to display your data in figures, charts, graphs, and tables.

Have Fun!

We hope you will use this book to design prize-winning science projects and to learn about science in general. It is also important, though, that you have fun! Let your creativity and curiosity guide you while you do these experiments. Good luck!

THE MANY FACES OF ACIDS AND BASES

Cabbage Juice pH Paper

You can make colored paper by changing pH, using cabbages and coffee filters.

This is what you'll need:

⅓ to ½ head red cabbage
A grater
A pot for boiling
Water
A strainer
A large bowl
6 paper cups
Lemon juice
2 tablespoons of baking soda dissolved in ½ cup water
Vinegar
Liquid laundry detergent (if you only have powdered detergent,
    dissolve 2 tablespoons in ½ cup water)
Milk
12 coffee filters
A cookie sheet

Safety Warning: Have an adult supervise when using the stove.

Here's what to do:

1. Grate the red cabbage into the pot.
2. Pour in enough water to cover the cabbage.
3. Boil the mixture for 30 minutes.
4. After you've boiled it, turn off the heat and let the mixture sit until it cools a bit (you don't need to handle boiling liquid). Strain the mixture into the bowl, using the strainer to remove all the cabbage. The liquid in the bowl should be dark bluish purple in color.
5. Test the cabbage juice to make sure it can detect pH:
    5A. Pour a small amount of cabbage juice into each of the six paper cups.
    5B. Pour a small amount of one test liquid into each cup. The test liquids should be: water, lemon juice, baking soda solution, vinegar, laundry detergent solution, and milk. Label the cups so you know which test liquid was added to each cup.
    5C. Record any changes you notice in the color of the cabbage juice.

5D. Dip the coffee filters in the cabbage juice so they soak through and then let them dry on a cookie sheet.

5E. When the filters are dry, you can cut them into strips so you have more samples.

What you should notice:

◆ When you mix the cabbage juice with an acidic solution, it should turn bright pink.

◆ When you mix the cabbage juice with a basic solution, it should turn green.

Here's what's happening:

Scientists define acids and bases in relation to the balance of protons and electrons in the solution. Protons and electrons are particles found inside atoms, which are the building blocks of chemicals. Protons have a positive charge and electrons have a negative charge.

Some solutions have an excess of protons; these solutions are acidic. Acids have a pH below 7. Neutral solutions, where there are equal amounts of protons and electrons, have a pH of exactly 7. Basic solutions have an excess of electrons, and they have a pH above 7.

Red cabbage contains pigments called *anthocyanins*. Anthocyanin molecules are sensitive to pH—they change in color depending on the pH of their surroundings. The anthocyanins in red cabbage take on the colors listed in the box to the right at different pH values. Because of its ability to change color with pH, cabbage juice is considered a pH indicator.

pH	approximate color
2	Red
4	Purple
6	Violet
8	Blue
10	Green
12	Greenish-yellow

Dig a little deeper:

The pH scale is a measurement based on the concentration of protons in a solution. Hydrogen atoms contain one proton and one electron. When a hydrogen atom loses its electron, it becomes a hydrogen ion (a particle with a net positive or negative charge). A hydrogen ion (denoted by H+) is a single proton, so a solution with an excess of protons actually has an excess of H+ ions. The greater the concentration of H+ ions, the more acidic a solution is, and the lower its pH is. The lower the concentration of H+ ions, the more basic a solution is, and the higher its pH is.

Things to try:

→ Beets, cranberries, and blueberries also contain anthocyanins. Test the pH properties of these foods and compare them to cabbage juice.

Pink Breath
Is there something pink in your breath?

This is what you'll need:

Cabbage juice from "Cabbage Juice pH Paper" (see page 11)
A clear drinking glass
A straw

Here's what to do:

1. Pour some cabbage juice into the drinking glass.
2. Place the straw in the cabbage juice and gently blow some bubbles in the liquid. Keep blowing until the cabbage juice changes color.

What you should notice:

◆ After a few moments of blowing bubbles, the cabbage juice turns pink.

Here's what's happening:

You probably already know that there is a lot of carbon dioxide in the breath you exhale. What you may not know is that the carbon dioxide gas you exhale can be dissolved in liquids. In fact, pretty much all gases can dissolve in liquids—which is why fish can breathe underwater.

When carbon dioxide dissolves in water, a chemical reaction takes place producing carbonic acid. The presence of the acid is what changes the color of the cabbage juice indicator to pink.

Dig a little deeper:

Below is the actual reaction that takes place between the carbon dioxide and air:

$$CO_2 \quad + \quad H_2O \quad \longrightarrow \quad H_2CO_3$$
$$\text{Carbon dioxide} \quad + \quad \text{Water} \quad \longrightarrow \quad \text{Carbonic acid}$$

Only a very little bit of carbonic acid is produced in this way, but it is enough to lower the pH of the solution.

Basic Effects on Color
Does bleach turn everything white?

This is what you'll need:

Construction paper of different colors
A cookie sheet
Cotton swabs
Diluted chlorine bleach (¼ cup bleach mixed
    with ¼ cup water)
Diluted color-safe bleach (¼ cup bleach mixed
    with ¼ cup water)
*Safety Warning: Be careful when handling chemicals like bleach,
since direct contact can be harmful.*

Here's what to do:

1. Cut the construction paper so you have two 3-inch squares of each color.
2. Lay the squares out on the cookie sheet.
3. Dip a cotton swab in the diluted chlorine bleach. Touch each colored square with the bleach on the cotton swab.
4. Dip a cotton swab in the diluted color-safe bleach. Touch each colored square with the bleach on the cotton swab.
5. Record how the color changes in the chart on the next page.

What you should notice:

◆ When chlorine bleach is added to the construction paper, the color will lighten. Depending on the original dye, the paper may turn white or some intermediate color.
◆ Color-safe bleach also reacts with many of the pieces of colored construction paper, though to a different extent.

Here's what's happening:

Chlorine bleach is an example of a very strong base—chemically, it is sodium hypochlorite (NaOCl). Strong bases can have dramatic effects on dyes. Bleach will eventually turn any color white, but depending on the chemical structure of the original dye, it may take more or less bleach to effectively remove the color. For example, when treated with bleach, some maroon dyes initially turn a golden-yellow color.

Color-safe bleaches have a different chemical structure from chlorine bleach, so they react differently with dyes. When dissolved in water, color-safe bleach undergoes a chemical reaction that releases hydrogen peroxide, which in turn breaks up the dye molecules. This bleach is not as strong as chlorine bleach, and doesn't remove as many dyes—and is therefore considered color-safe.

In this experiment, you have shown one very important application of acid–base chemistry—laundering clothes—as well as exploring how different kinds of chemistry can be used to accomplish the same goal.

Things to try:

→ Compare the sensitivity to bleach of dyes in the same color family used in cloth versus paper. For example, place a drop of bleach on a piece of red paper and on a piece of red cloth and note the results.

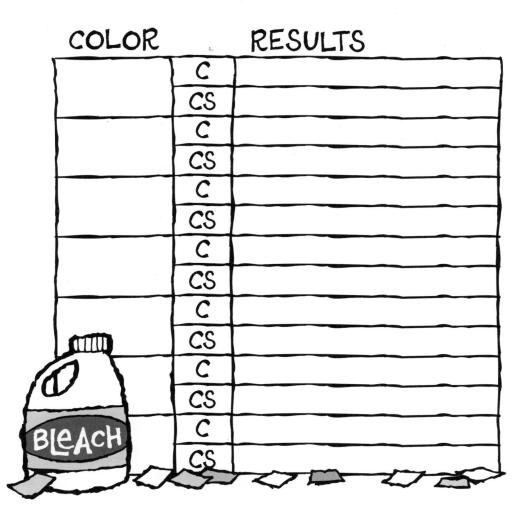

COLOR		RESULTS
	C	
	CS	
	C	
	CS	
	C	
	CS	
	C	
	CS	
	C	
	CS	
	C	
	CS	
	C	
	CS	

Leprechaun Soap

The perfect gift for the leprechaun in your life.

This is what you'll need:

A bar of white soap
Cabbage juice from "Cabbage Juice pH Paper" (see page 11)

Here's what to do:

1. Pour a thin layer of cabbage juice on the bar of soap. Record any color changes that occur.
2. Rub some cabbage juice on your hands. Let it dry.
3. Wash your hands with any soap. Record what happens to the soapy water as you rinse.

What you should notice:

◆ When cabbage juice is poured on the bar of soap, it slowly turns green.
◆ When you wash the dried cabbage juice off your hands with soap, the soapy water turns green.

Here's what's happening:

One of the main ingredients of soap is some kind of basic substance, usually sodium hydroxide or potassium hydroxide. The pH of most hand soaps falls someplace between 8.5 and 10. Since the soap is basic, it is able to change to color of the cabbage juice indicator green when the two come into contact.

Why You Can't Bleach Sheep
Why does bleach turn wool to goo?

This is what you'll need:

A scrap of wool fabric
½ cup chlorine bleach
A glass jar

Safety Warning: Be careful when handling chemicals like bleach, since direct contact can be harmful.

Here's what to do:

1. Combine the fabric scrap and the bleach in the glass jar. If there isn't enough liquid to cover the fabric, add water.
2. Wait five minutes and then examine the fabric from the outside of the jar. *Do not touch the fabric.* Record your observations.

What you should notice:

◆ Instead of turning the whool white, the bleach turns the fabric into a yellow, gooey mess.

Here's what's happening:

As explained in "Basic Effects on Color" (see page 14), chlorine bleach is a strong base. When bleach reacts with fibers like cotton, it bleaches well. This is because both bleach and cotton are on the basic side of the pH scale. Wool, on the other hand, is an acidic fiber. When wool is combined with bleach, a chemical reaction called a *neutralization reaction* takes place. The result is that the bleach dissolves the wool into yellow goo. You can compare the reaction of bleach with wool and the reaction of bleach with cotton by repeating this experiment using a cotton scrap instead of a wool scrap.

Dig a little deeper:

When wool is prepared commercially, it is treated in a variety of ways to make bleaching possible. For example, the wool is soaked in acid before and after the bleaching process. The extra acid helps neutralize the pH and prevents the bleach from dissolving the wool.

Warning: At home, you should never combine an acidic liquid with chlorine bleach—you could release potentially dangerous gases in the process.

Things to try:

→ Human hair is also acidic. What does bleach do to hair? How do you think drain cleaners work?

Acid Rain
Are the water sources around you safe?

This is what you'll need:

- Red and blue litmus paper (from a science supply store)
- A cookie sheet
- An eyedropper
- Rainwater (you can collect some rainwater in a cup placed on your lawn or outside on your windowsill)
- Tap water (collected fresh from the tap)
- Distilled water
- Pond water

Here's what to do:

1. Lay out the red and blue litmus paper on a cookie sheet.
2. Using the eyedropper, place one drop of rainwater on each piece of litmus paper. Record any color changes you see. Wash out the eyedropper afterward.
3. Repeat this process for the tap water, distilled water, and pond water samples, by placing a drop of each sample on both types of litmus paper.
4. Record any color changes you observe.

What you should notice:

◆ The samples will change the color of the litmus paper differently, based on their pH values.

Here's what's happening:

People usually assume that water has a neutral pH, but water can have all sorts of dissolved impurities that change its pH, sometimes significantly. For example, tap water fresh from the tap is often slightly basic (changing the red litmus paper to blue), because it can have a lot of dissolved carbon dioxide in it. If you didn't use a sample fresh from the tap, you may not have seen this effect, because as tap water sits, it becomes more "flat" as the carbon dioxide leaves. This is the same effect as you get when carbonated soda is left out.

Distilled water usually has neutral pH (and doesn't change the color of either type of litmus paper). The pH of pond water can fluctuate greatly and is often chemically adjusted by caretakers to prevent dangerous conditions.

Rainwater is also normally on the acidic side, turning the blue litmus paper red. There are many pollutants and oxides in the air, including carbon dioxide, that get caught in rainwater as it falls. Unpolluted rainwater has a pH of approximately 5.6, but pH values below 5 can be harmful for plants and wildlife. In the United States, the most acidic rainwater has been recorded at a pH of 4.3.

Things to try:

→ Test water from a swimming pool, a public fountain, and parking lot puddles. What do you notice about the pH values? What accounts for any differences you see?

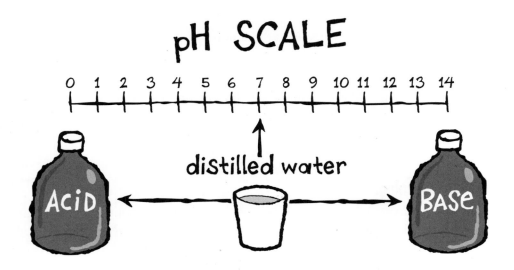

Turmeric Indicator
Another way to color your bases (and acids).

This is what you'll need:

½ teaspoon turmeric
½ cup rubbing alcohol
A bowl
1 teaspoon baking soda
¼ cup water
A clear drinking glass
¼ cup vinegar

Safety Warning: Be careful when handling alcohol. It is flamable and direct contact can be harmful.

Here's what to do:

1. Mix the turmeric and rubbing alcohol in the bowl.
2. Mix the water and baking soda in the drinking glass.
3. Pour some of the turmeric–alcohol mixture into the drinking glass, just enough to cause the liquids to change colors. Record what kind of color change occurs.
4. Slowly pour the vinegar into the drinking glass, recording what happens to the liquids.

What you should notice:

◆ When you add the turmeric-alcohol mixture to the baking soda solution in the drinking glass, the solution turns red.
◆ When you add the vinegar to the liquid in the drinking glass, the solution will foam and turn yellow.

Here's what's happening:

A *pH indicator* is a chemical substance that changes in some way depending on the pH it encounters. Often, pH indicators change colors to indicate acidic or basic solutions. The turmeric-alcohol mixture is a pH indicator in the same way that the cabbage juice is, but it has different properties. In acidic solutions, the mixture stays yellow; in basic solutions, the mixture turns red.

In this experiment, you show that the color change of the indicator is reversible. The baking soda is basic, and initially adding the turmeric–alcohol mixture to the baking soda solution causes a color change to red. When you add vinegar to the drinking glass, at first, the acidic vinegar reacts with the baking soda, neutralizing it. The bubbles you see are from the carbon dioxide produced during the neutralization reaction. Eventually, you add more vinegar than necessary to neutralize the baking soda, and the solution becomes acidic, causing the turmeric indicator to change back to a yellow color.

Things to try:

→ Test how the turmeric indicator compares to the cabbage juice indicator. Soak one end of several cotton swabs in the turmeric–alcohol mixture for 3 minutes. Leave the cotton swabs to dry on a cookie sheet. The dried cotton swabs can be dipped into liquids to check pH.

Dracula Soap
Don't forget a gift for your favorite vampire.

This is what you'll need:

A bar of white soap
Turmeric-alcohol mixture from "Turmeric Indicator" (see page 20)

Here's what to do:

1. Pour a thin layer of turmeric indicator on the bar of soap. Record any color changes that occur.
2. Rub some turmeric indicator on your hands. Let it dry.
3. Wash your hands with any soap. Record what happens to the soapy water as you rinse.

What you should notice:

◆ When turmeric indicator is poured on the bar of soap, it slowly turns red.
◆ When you wash the dried turmeric indicator off your hands with soap, the soapy water turns red.

Here's what's happening:

Just like in the "Leprechaun Soap" experiment on page 16, the pH of the soap changes the color of the turmeric indicator. Because turmeric and cabbage juice have different color properties when in contact with basic substances, they look very different at the end of the experiment. Nevertheless, the underlying principles are the same: the basic soap reacts with the pH indicator and produces a visible color change.

Shiny New Pennies
Make your pennies bright as new!

This is what you'll need:

Water

Dish soap

2 drinking glasses

½ cup lemon juice

1 teaspoon table salt

Some dull, dirty pennies

Here's what to do:

1. Pour some water and dish soap into one glass. Get the soap all sudsy.
2. Pour the lemon juice and the table salt in the other glass.
3. Add a few dull, dirty pennies to each glass.
4. Let the pennies soak for five minutes, and then take them out and rinse them well in running water. Examine their appearance.

What you should notice:

◆ The pennies in the soapy water look just as dull and dirty after soaking and rinsing.
◆ The pennies in the lemon juice look bright and shiny after soaking and rinsing.

Here's what's happening:

American pennies are coated with copper, which can react with the oxygen in the air to form copper oxide. Copper oxide looks dull and dirty when it covers a penny. You can chemically remove the copper oxide by submerging the pennies in a solution of acid and salt. In this case, the lemon juice is the acid.

Because the lemon juice is acidic, it has an excess of H^+ ions (see "Cabbage Juice pH Paper" on page 11 for the explanation). Below is the chemical reaction between the copper oxide and the H^+ ions:

$$CuO\,(solid) \quad + \quad H^+ \quad \longrightarrow \quad Cu^{2+} \quad + \quad H_2O$$

$$Copper\ oxide \quad + \quad H^+ \quad \longrightarrow \quad Copper\ ions \quad + \quad Water$$

The acid essentially dissolves the solid copper oxide into copper ions and water. The salt that you added speeds up the reaction.

Things to try:

→ Other acids can dissolve copper oxide as well. Try other household acids and compare how well they clean the pennies.

Green Pennies
Can lemon juice make pennies turn green too?

This is what you'll need:

½ cup lemon juice
1 teaspoon table salt
A drinking glass
Some dull, dirty pennies

Here's what to do:

1. Pour the lemon juice and the table salt in the glass.
2. Add a few dull, dirty pennies.
3. Let the pennies soak for five minutes. Then take them out and let them dry on a paper towel. Leave them alone overnight.
4. The next day, examine the pennies and record any changes in their appearance.

What you should notice:

◆ A blue-green solid should cover the pennies.

Here's what's happening:

In "Shiny New Pennies" on page 23, you used lemon juice to clean old pennies, but in this experiment, a similar setup creates pennies covered in a green coating. How can the same chemicals create two different results?

The last step of "Shiny New Pennies" was rinsing the soaked pennies in running water. In this experiment, you don't rinse the pennies; instead, the lemon juice and salt are allowed to dry on the pennies. This is what creates the difference in results. The lemon juice–salt mixture again serves to dissolve the copper oxide. However, without rinsing, a second chemical reaction takes place. The copper atoms react with oxygen from the air and chlorine from the salt to create a blue-green compound called malachite.

Dig a little deeper:

Malachite is one of the oldest known green pigments. More than 6,000 years ago, ancient Egyptians used malachite as makeup. Around AD 900, the ancient Chinese began using ground malachite mixed with water to make paint for paintings.

Apples and Oranges

Keep an apple from browning using an orange.

This is what you'll need:

An apple, cut in half
A round orange slice

Here's what to do:

1. Place the slice of orange over the white part of one apple half.
2. Leave the other half uncovered.
3. Leave the fruit out for two hours, and then record any differences in appearance you observe.

What you should notice:

◆ The uncovered apple half will turn brown.
◆ The apple half covered in the orange slice will be free of browning.

Here's what's happening:

Each apple cell contains a chemical called *polyphenol oxidase* (PPO). When an apple is sliced, some of the cells are opened and the PPO is exposed to the air. This exposure allows PPO to react with the oxygen in the air in a process called *oxidation*. This is what makes the apple slices turn brown.

One way to prevent oxidation is to prevent oxygen from reaching the PPO molecules in the cells. Do this by submerging the apple slices in water or by wrapping them tightly in plastic wrap. Alternatively, you can add ascorbic acid (also known as vitamin C) to the apples to prevent the chemical reaction from taking place.

Orange juice contains a lot of ascorbic acid. Placing the apple half in contact with the orange slice introduces ascorbic acid into the apple cells. In addition, the orange slice acts as a barrier to air, preventing oxygen from reaching the PPO molecules. This prevents the apple from browning.

Dig a little deeper:

Another way to prevent apples from browning is to cook them, since heat breaks up the molecules that are involved in the browning reaction, preventing it from taking place.

Things to try:

→ Compare the effects of coating the apple slice in orange juice and covering it with an orange slice. Which is better at preventing browning?
→ Lime juice, lemon juice, and pineapple juice also contain ascorbic acid. Which is best at preventing the browning of the apple slices?

Marble Measure
What's in those rocks in your backyard?

This is what you'll need:

Marble gravel (available in gardening supply stores)
A small piece of limestone (available in gardening
    supply stores)
A small piece of slate (available in gardening
    supply stores)
Small rocks from your neighborhood
Several clear drinking glasses large enough to
    hold the rock samples you collected (you can
    use bowls if the samples are too large to fit
    in a glass)
White vinegar

Here's what to do:

1. Label the glasses "Marble," "Limestone," "Slate," and "Neighborhood Rocks."
2. Place the rocks in the appropriate glasses.
3. Pour vinegar into each glass to completely cover the rocks.
4. Observe what happens in each glass. Record your observations.

What you should notice:

◆ Bubbles appear in the glass containing marble.
◆ Bubbles appear in the glass containing limestone.
◆ There is no reaction in the glass containing slate.
◆ Depending on the makeup of the neighborhood rocks, you may or may not see bubbles.

Here's what's happening:

Marble and limestone, and many other rocks, contain a chemical compound called *calcium carbonate*. When calcium carbonate comes into contact with an acidic substance—like vinegar—a chemical reaction takes place. The bubbles are the evidence of the chemical reaction. Slate does not contain calcium carbonate, so it does not react with the vinegar at all.

The actual chemical reaction between the calcium carbonate and vinegar (acetic acid) produces calcium acetate (a soluble salt water) and carbon dioxide gas. The bubbles you see are from the carbon dioxide gas.

Dig a little deeper:

Many ancient buildings, like those made by the ancient Romans or Greeks, were made out of marble. The deterioration of these buildings over time is increased because of natural phenomena like acid rain.

Things to try:

➔ Other things, like bones and seashells, contain calcium carbonate. Submerge these in vinegar and see what you get.

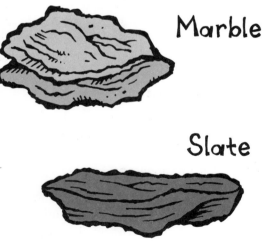

Marble

Limestone

Slate

THE SCIENCE OF LIFE

Planet of Planaria
Go fishing for some special worms.

This is what you'll need:

A small jar
Access to a pond
A small piece of raw chicken liver
A nylon stocking
A magnifying glass

Safety Warning: **Always** *remember to wash your hands thoroughly with soap and warm water after handling raw meat.*

Here's what to do:

1. Collect some clear pond water in the jar. Make sure you don't collect too much mud or other stuff that makes the water cloudy, since you will need to see things in the water.
2. Put the chicken liver inside the nylon stocking.
3. Go "fishing" in the pond with the chicken liver as bait.
4. After three minutes, gently dip the chicken liver into the jar of pond water.
5. Examine the water with a magnifying glass. Did you catch any planaria?

What you should notice:

◆ The chicken liver should have attracted small swimming critters that are visible with a magnifying glass.

Here's what's happening:

Planaria are tiny, meat-eating flatworms that live in ponds. Part of their job is to clean up the pond by feeding on dead animals. They detect food using their sense of smell. In this experiment, the raw chicken liver attracted the planaria, and then you were able to "fish" them out in the nylon stocking.

When you looked closely at the planaria, you may have noticed two small "eyes" on each of their heads. Planaria cannot see the way we see—instead of seeing complete pictures of the world, their eyes can only sense light areas versus dark areas. Another interesting thing about these worms is that if you cut one in half, each half is able to regenerate a whole healthy worm.

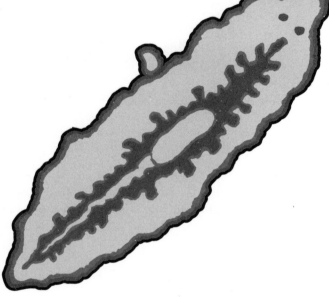

Things to try:

➔ Using an eyedropper, transfer some planaria into a petri dish. Cover half of the petri dish with foil and leave everything in direct sunlight. Take the foil off after five minutes. Were the planaria attracted to the light side or the dark side of the dish?

Cell Staining
Color your cellular world.

This is what you'll need:

Tweezers
An onion
Glass microscope slides and cover slips
3 eyedroppers (for water, iodine, and methylene blue)
Water
Iodine (available at drugstores)
Methylene blue (available at aquarium supply stores)
Paper towels
Toothpicks
A microscope

Safety Warning: Be careful when handling chemicals like iodine and methylene blue, since direct contact can be harmful.

Here's what to do:

Onion Cells:

1. Use the tweezers to tear off a thin layer of the onion's skin—the thinner, the better!
2. Lay the skin flat on the microscope slide.
3. Repeat the previous two steps twice so you have three onion skin slides.
4. Use the eyedropper to place a small drop of water over each piece of onion skin.
5. Carefully place a cover slip over the water and onion skin on each slide, trying to avoid leaving air bubbles under the cover slip.
6. On the first slide, place a small drop of iodine on one corner of the cover slip. On the second slide, place a small drop of methylene blue. The stain will mix with the water and slowly seep under the cover slip. Leave the third slide without any stain.
7. Soak up any excess liquid carefully with a paper towel.

Cells from Inside Your Cheek:

1. Use the toothpick to gently scrape the inside of your mouth under your cheek.
2. Gently rub the end of the toothpick that was in your mouth on a microscope slide.
3. Repeat the previous two steps twice so you have three cheek cell slides.
4. Use the eyedropper to place a small drop of water on each slide, roughly on the same spot where you rubbed the toothpick on the slide.
5. Carefully place a cover slip over the water and cells on each slide.

6. As before, place a small drop of iodine on one corner of one cover slip and a small drop of methylene blue on another slip. Leave the third slide without any stain.
7. Soak up any excess liquid carefully with a paper towel.
8. Place the slides one by one under the microscope and examine them at different magnifications.

What you should notice:

◆ When the onion skin cells or the cheek cells are stained, the nucleus and cell membranes are more visible.
◆ The onion skin cells have a cell wall, whereas the cheek cells do not.
◆ At high magnifications, you might be able to detect motion inside the cells in the part called the cytoplasm.

Here's what's happening:

Almost all living cells share the following parts: a nucleus (usually one of the largest structures inside the cell), which is the "control center" of the cell; a nuclear membrane that separates the nucleus from the rest of the cell; a cell membrane that separates the cell from other things; and the cytoplasm, which is the material inside the cell membrane. These structures are usually easily visible under a microscope. Other structures you may have seen are the mitochondria, which are the structures that make energy for the cell, and chloroplasts (in plant cells only), which are small green structures that hold chlorophyll. Plant cells also have an outer cell wall, which is identifiable by its rigid structure.

Most of the time, cells look pretty transparent when viewed through a microscope. Scientists have developed a number of stains to help view cells more clearly. Some of these stains only color certain types of cells; others only color certain parts of cells. Many stains are only safe to use in a laboratory, but iodine and methylene blue can be effectively used at home. When you stained the onion skin or the cheek cells with either iodine or methylene blue, you probably noticed that some structures like the nucleus and cell membranes became especially visible. You probably also noticed that one stain works better on one type of cell than the other.

If you weren't able to see anything through the microscope, you may not have been at a high enough magnification, or you may have used too much stain.

Dig a little deeper:

Try to identify the following in the cells you observe:

Nucleus
Nuclear membrane
Cytoplasm
Cell membrane
Cell wall (plants only)
Chloroplasts (plants only)
Mitochondria

Things to try:

→ Study other samples like paper-thin slices of potato or cork. What similarities and differences do you notice?

→ Try other things as cell stains, like food coloring or grape juice. Do these work? What cell strctures get stained?

Spinach DNA
Can you extract DNA from your salad?

This is what you'll need:

About ½ cup fresh spinach
¼ teaspoon table salt
1 cup cold water
A blender
A strainer
A clear glass measuring cup
2 tablespoons dish detergent
Meat tenderizer
Rubbing alcohol

Safety Warning: Be careful when handling chemicals like rubbing alcohol, since direct contact can be harmful.

Here's what to do:

1. Add the spinach, salt, and water to the blender and blend on high for 30 seconds, or until you have a pretty uniform spinach soup.
2. Pour the spinach soup through the strainer into the measuring cup.
3. Add the dish detergent to the strained spinach soup. Let this mixture stand for 10 minutes.
4. Add a pinch of meat tenderizer to the measuring cup. Mix very gently but thoroughly.
5. Check the volume of the solution in the measuring cup. Slowly and gently add an equal amount of rubbing alcohol.
6. Let the solution sit for a few minutes. Look for a stringy white film—this is the DNA.

What you should notice:

◆ When you add the alcohol, the resulting solution gets a bit cloudy.

Here's what's happening:

DNA is the basic building block of all life. It is the blueprint that organisms use to figure out how to be what they are. Scientists are able to collect DNA from any living thing. This experiment shows a way you can collect the DNA from some spinach. (You can actually use any living material to extract DNA with this method. But since you had to blend it to get at the DNA, it probably was not a good idea to use things like live animals or your little brother.)

To be able to collect the DNA from the spinach cells, a number of things have to happen. First, you have to break up the spinach into individual cells, which you did by blending it. Then the detergent helps to break open the cells to make the DNA easy to get to. A DNA strand is incredibly small, so you cannot isolate it by itself—you have to find a way to make a lot of DNA strands stick together to make them easier to purify. This is where the alcohol helps. There is a chemical reaction between the DNA and the alcohol that makes all of the DNA strands stick together. As long as you keep the DNA you collected in alcohol, it will remain white and stringy.

Dig a little deeper:

DNA is found in the nucleus of a cell. Cells generally have an outer cell membrane, which keeps everything in, and a nucleus, which contains DNA and other proteins and is surrounded by a nuclear membrane. (To learn more about cells, go to "Cell Staining" on page 30.) Think of the DNA as being double-bagged—first by the nuclear membrane and then by the cell membrane. When you blend the spinach, what you are really doing is separating the spinach cells, so that the DNA in each of the cells is more accessible. The detergent is used to break open the two membranes so that the DNA is in the solution rather than protected inside the cell.

The meat tenderizer that you add has enzymes in it. In this experiment, you need the enzymes to help purify the DNA. Inside a cell, in addition to the DNA in the nucleus, there are also carbohydrates and tons of proteins. In fact, there are proteins all tangled up with the DNA. When you try to purify the DNA, you have to get rid of the proteins somehow.

The enzymes in the meat tenderizer help to cut up the extra proteins like a pair of scissors.

DNA stands for "deoxyribonucleic acid," which means that DNA is an acid. Each strand of DNA has a slightly negative charge. When you add the alcohol to get the white DNA film, what you are really doing taking the DNA out of solution and changing it into solid form. This is called precipitating the acid. In order to do this, there has to be enough salt in the solution to keep the individual DNA strands from repelling each other. The alcohol is there to separate the water in the solution from the DNA. The result is the white precipitated DNA.

Believe it or not, the principles used here to get DNA from spinach are the same ones used by the pros—they just have better equipment. Scientists collect DNA from different sources to help them study the biology of different organisms. For example, the DNA from viruses is collected and studied when making new vaccines. Scientists study the DNA from cancer cells and compare it with normal cells to try to figure out how to treat cancer.

Things to try:

→ Use different DNA sources, like chicken liver, onions, or peas. What gives you the most DNA?

→ Try different detergents, like laundry detergent or bath soap. Does this make a difference?

→ Leave out the salt. Do you still get DNA at the end?

Oily Feathers

Explore why oil spills are so harmful to wildlife.

This is what you'll need:

A feather	A bowl
Water	Liquid soap
Vegetable oil	A toothbrush

Here's what to do:

1. Sprinkle a few drops of water on the feather. Record whether the water is absorbed or if the feather repels the water in the chart on the next page.
2. Pour a small amount of vegetable oil on the feather so it has a thin coat of oil on it. Record in the chart how the feather changes because of the oil.
3. Sprinkle water on the oily feather. Record whether the water is absorbed or if the feather repels the water in the chart.
4. Pour some water into the bowl and add a few drops of liquid soap. Try to clean the oil off the feather using the toothbrush and the soapy water.
5. Record in the chart any differences you notice in the feather after you've tried to clean it.

What you should notice:

◆ Normally, the feather is able to repel water.
◆ When the feather gets coated in oil, the weight of the oil causes the feather to droop.
◆ The oily feather is not able to repel water.
◆ Even after you try to wash the feather in soap, it doesn't really return to being the way it was before the oil coating.

Here's what's happening:

If you look closely, you will see that each feather is made of individual strands that are bound together by tiny hooks arranged in rows. When feathers are in good condition, they keep the bird warm and dry. Oil clogs the arrangement of strands and hooks on each feather, and the feather loses its ability to repel water. Also, when the feathers are not in good shape, the bird loses the layer of insulating air between its skin and feathers that the feathers usually keep in. The bird is left without protection against rain and cold weather. This can dramatically reduce the bird's ability to survive.

In this experiment, you used vegetable oil, which is considerably easier to clean up than the crude oil carried in tankers on the oceans. When there is an oil spill, people have to take responsibility and clean off the wildlife that got caught in the spill. As you saw, however, it is difficult to properly clean oil off a bird's feathers. This is why it is important that we protect the environment and prevent disasters like oil spills.

Dig a little deeper:

This experiment demonstrates well why oil spills are so harmful to the environment. In addition to hurting the feathers of birds caught in the spill, oil is often toxic. Animals that try to clean themselves of oil by licking their fur, feathers, or skin can become poisoned by ingesting the oil.

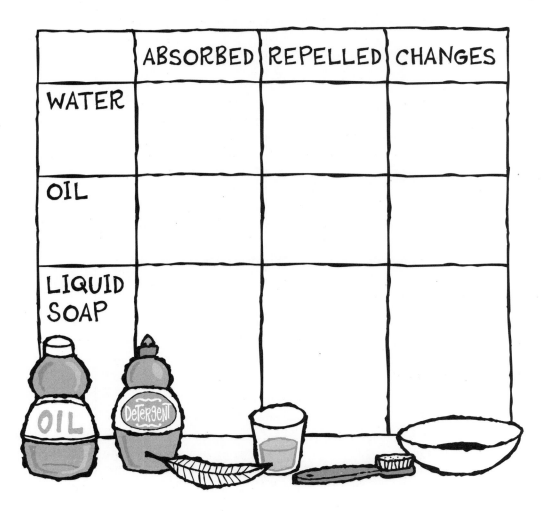

	ABSORBED	REPELLED	CHANGES
WATER			
OIL			
LIQUID SOAP			

Earthworm Garden
See for yourself what earthworms do to soil.

This is what you'll need:

A large jar with a lid
Potting soil
Cornstarch
Apple peelings
A marker
2 or 3 earthworms (which can be found by
        digging in your yard or at a bait store)
Safety Warning: Since you are working with live animals,
use care to prevent hurting them.

Here's what to do:

1. Make sure the jar is clean before you start.
2. Fill the jar with alternating layers of soil and cornstarch. The soil layers can be thicker than the cornstarch layers. Make sure you have at least four layers total.
3. Place a layer of apple peelings at the top.
4. On the outside of the jar, use the marker to mark the boundaries between each layer.
5. Place the earthworms in the jar on top of all the layers.
6. Loosely replace the lid on the jar.
7. Observe the earthworm garden every day. Record what happens to the layers of soil, cornstarch, and apple peelings.
8. Make sure you water the earthworm garden every day to keep the soil moist.

What you should notice:

◆ Over time, the movement of the earthworms mixes up all the layers in the jar.
◆ The total height of the materials in the jar gets reduced over time.

Here's what's happening:

When earthworms burrow through soil, they are looking for food to eat. The result of their movement is to create little tunnels through the soil. This is beneficial for plants, because the soil they grow in becomes better aerated by the worm tunnels. Earthworms also eat organic materials (like the apple peelings in this experiment) and then excrete worm castings that may be seen in your earthworm garden as a thick black layer of dirt. The worm cast material has a different makeup from the soil and is often denser and heavier than soil. This material also returns some nutrients from the apple peelings to the soil faster than waiting for the apple peelings to decompose.

The purpose of the alternating layers of soil and cornstarch is to dramatically show how much motion a few little worms create. After a few weeks, the soil will appear almost homogeneous, except, of course, for the black worm cast that is probably sitting near the top. Because the worm cast material is denser than soil, it weighs everything down. The motion of the worms serves to pack the soil down, so the height of the worm garden reduces over time.

Why You Don't Go Barefoot

How many times have your parents told you, "Don't walk barefoot in the grass"? In this experiment, you can find out why.

This is what you'll need:

3 pairs of clean socks
6 plastic containers
A grassy field
Water
Hand soap
An eyedropper
A microscope (preferred, but a magnifying glass
    will do if you don't have a microscope)
Slides for a microscope

Here's what to do:

1. Place two of the socks into plastic containers (one sock in each container) at the beginning of the experiment. Label these containers "Control."

2. Put on the second pair of socks and walk through a grassy field in your socks.

3. Repeat with the third pair of socks.

4. Place two of the dirty socks into plastic containers (one sock in each container). Add some water to each container. Label these containers "Dirty Socks."

5. Wash the remaining dirty socks with some hand soap. Don't wash them too much; pretend you are washing your hands after being outside. Place each sock into a plastic container, and add some water. Label these containers "Washed Socks."

6. Group together one container from each pair. Place one group in direct sunlight and the other group in the shade.

7. Watch what happens to the socks over the next week. Record your observations every day.

8. After a week, label six slides "Control—Sun," "Dirty Socks—Sun," "Washed Socks—Sun," "Control—Shade," "Dirty Socks—Shade," and "Washed Socks—Shade."

9. Use an eyedropper to suck out some water from the containers. Make sure you match up the correct container to the correct slide and that you wash out the eyedropper well between containers.

10. View the water drops under a microscope. (If you don't have a microscope, use a magnifying glass. You won't be able to see as much, but you should still be able to detect some critters in the water.) Record your observations and make drawings of anything you see.

What you should notice:

◆ The "Dirty Socks" should have many small plants growing on them. Water drops from these containers should have small critters swimming around.

◆ The "Washed Socks" may have some small plants growing on them. Water drops from these containers may have a few small critters swimming around.

◆ The "Control" socks should not have any small plants growing on them. Water drops from these containers should not have any small critters swimming around.

◆ You may notice that the types of swimming critters you see in the samples left in sunlight are different from those in the samples left in shade.

Here's what's happening:

There are all sorts of things in the grass and in the dirt that you may not normally see. This experiment helps you focus on those unseen critters.

You may have noticed small plants growing on the "Dirty Socks." Many types of grasses make seeds that are designed to be able to hook onto passing feet, fur, or clothing. This design helps to spread the grass seeds far and wide. For example, carried on your socks, the seeds made it all the way inside your house. Things like wind or rain would not have been able to distribute the seeds that far. By giving their seeds the ability to "move," these grasses help ensure their survival.

Mud and dirt are also popular places for tiny organisms to live. One type of organism, called protozoa, consists of single-celled animals that are commonly found in dirt. The swimming critters from the "Dirty Socks" water were different types of protozoa. Since different protozoa need different conditions to thrive, you may have noticed variations in the types of protozoa in the water left in the sun and the water left in the shade.

You may have noticed that there are still plants and protozoa growing on the washed socks. Some seeds and protozoa can hang on pretty tenaciously—which makes sense, since the animal they've attached themselves to may get a little "washed" by walking through a stream or through the rain. By figuring out how to hang on, these seeds and protozoa increase their ability to move to new areas.

Things to try:

→ See how long the seeds and microorganisms that latch onto your socks can survive before you let them grow in water. Walk around in your socks and then place them individually inside two plastic bags. Put one bag in the freezer and the other one in a dark place at room temperature (for example, the bottom of a closet). After a week, take the socks out and put them in water as you did above. Does anything grow?

Algae Farming
What conditions give you the best algae harvest?

This is what you'll need:

5 glass jars with lids
Tap water
Pond water
A marker
Copper sulfate crystals (from a science
    supply store)
Dry lawn fertilizer
Powdered laundry detergent
Vegetable oil

Safety Warning: Be careful when handling chemicals like
fertilizer and copper sulfate, since direct contact can be harmful.

Here's what to do:

1. Wash and dry the jars well, making sure there is no soap left in them once they are rinsed.
2. Add 2 cups of tap water to each jar.
3. Stir the pond water well and then add 5 tablespoons of pond water to each jar.
4. Loosely cover one jar with its lid, and use the marker to label it "Pond Water Only."
5. Add 2 tablespoons of copper sulfate crystals to the second jar. Loosely cover this jar with its lid, and use the marker to label it "Copper Sulfate."
6. Add 2 tablespoons of dry lawn fertilizer to the third jar. Loosely cover this jar with its lid, and use the marker to label it "Fertilizer."
7. Add 2 tablespoons of powdered laundry detergent to the fourth jar. Loosely cover this jar with its lid, and use the marker to label it "Detergent."
8. Add 2 tablespoons of vegetable oil to the fifth jar. Loosely cover this jar with its lid, and use the marker to label it "Oil." Examine the jar to see to see how much of the water's surface is covered by the oil.
9. Set all the jars in direct sunlight. Observe the jars every day for 2 weeks. Record any changes in the color of the water or anything you notice growing in it.

What you should notice:

- ◆ The jar marked "Copper Sulfate" will have little algae growth as compared with "Pond Water Only."
- ◆ The jar marked "Fertilizer" will have a lot of algae growth as compared with "Pond Water Only."
- ◆ The jar marked "Detergent" will have a lot of algae growth as compared with "Pond Water Only."
- ◆ The jar marked "Oil" will have little algae growth as compared with "Pond Water Only."

Here's what's happening:

Algae is actually a collection of small photosynthetic plants that growth in water. Pond water is full of algae. As long as conditions are favorable, algae from a little bit of pond water can grow in a jar of fresh water. In very little time, water that started clear can get green and cloudy from all the algae in it.

Certain chemicals can hurt or help the growth of algae. The copper in copper sulfate is very effective in killing algae; in fact, it is often used as an algicide. Algae grows well in high-nitrate or high-phosphate conditions. Fertilizer is high in nitrates; laundry detergent is high in phosphates. In both those jars, the algae probably grew faster.

The layer of oil in the fifth jar cuts off carbon dioxide to the water—since the oil layer floats on top of the water, the water is not able to have contact with air and is therefore unable to get carbon dioxide from the air. This reduces the amount of algae growth you see. Of course, if the oil you added was not enough to cover the surface of the water, algae growth may not have been affected. Examine the jar to make sure you know what the oil layer looked like to be able to correctly analyze the results.

Dig a little deeper:

Algae also grows well in iron-rich environments and in places with a lot of sunlight. Experiment with other materials from around the house to see what helps and what hurts your algae farm.

Things to try:

- → Algae depends on photosynthesis for energy. What happens to a jar of algae left in the dark?
- → Try varying the pH of the water. What is the best pH for algae farming?

Learning Worms
Can you train your pet earthworm?

This is what you'll need:

Paper towels

2 disposable foil dishes (you only need one at
      a time, but having two makes transferring
      the worm between steps easier)

Water

Rubber gloves for handling the earthworm and
      for protection from the butanol

An earthworm

2 syringes or eyedroppers

Rose oil (can be purchased at a drugstore
      or a specialty shop)

Butanol (can be purchased at science supply stores)

*Safety Warning: Since you are working with a live animal, use care
to prevent hurting it. Also, be careful when handling chemicals like
butanol, since direct contact can be harmful.*

Here's what to do:

1. Place a paper towel at the bottom of each of the foil dishes. Wet the paper towels with some water. You will need several more fresh paper towels for this experiment.
2. Wearing the rubber gloves, place the earthworm inside one dish.
3. Label one syringe (or eyedropper) "Rose Oil" and the other "Butanol." Fill each syringe appropriately.
4. Find the spot where the worm's body seems to be thickened or swollen. This spot is called the clitellum. The end closest to the clitellum is the worm's head.
5. Place one drop of rose oil near the worm's head. Record how the worm reacts.
6. Transfer the worm into the other foil dish on a fresh, damp paper towel.
7. Place one drop of butanol near the worm's head. Record how the worm reacts.
8. Transfer the worm into the other foil dish on a fresh, damp paper towel.
9. Hold the syringes close to the worm's head. Place one drop of rose oil near the worm's head and then one second later place one drop of butanol near the worm's head. Record how the worm reacts.
10. Transfer the worm back into the first foil dish on a fresh, damp paper towel.

11. Wait one minute. Then repeat the step where one drop of rose oil is quickly followed by one drop of butanol five times, recording the worm's reaction and transferring it onto a fresh, damp paper towel after each trial.
12. After you've performed the trial five or six times with a minute between each trial, place the worm on a fresh, damp paper towel and place one drop of butanol near the worm's head. Record how the worm reacts.
13. Transfer the worm into the other foil dish on a fresh, damp paper towel.
14. Place one drop of rose oil near the worm's head. Record how the worm reacts.

What you should notice:

◆ The first time you place a drop of rose oil near the worm's head, the worm doesn't really react.
◆ The first time you place a drop of butanol near the worm's head, the worm retracts its head in response.
◆ When the butanol drop quickly follows the rose oil drop, the worm retracts its head each time.
◆ After all the trials of rose oil followed by butanol, a drop of either liquid by itself causes the worm to retract its head.

Here's what's happening:

This experiment is an example of how scientists study the mechanisms of learning in animals. The smell of the rose oil is something that is not unpleasant to the worm; dropping rose oil near the worm's head doesn't make the worm recoil. On the other hand, butanol smells awful to a worm—as you could tell from the way the worm retracted every time you dropped butanol near its head.

By dropping rose oil directly followed by butanol, you were teaching the worm to associate the scent of the rose oil with the scent of the butanol. After a while, the worm had "learned" to associate either smell with something unpleasant. That is why after five or six learning trials, the worm began retracting its head in response to the rose oil by itself. Basically, the worm was pretty sure, based on its previous experience, that the smell of the rose oil would quickly become the awful smell of butanol, and it started retracting its head in anticipation. Pretty smart for an earthworm!

Dig a little deeper:

This type of learning experiment is known as *classical conditioning*, where a stimulus that produces a natural response (in this case, the worm retracting its head in response to the smell of butanol) that can be experimentally measured is paired with a stimulus that does not produce a noticeable response (in this case, the worm's reaction to the rose oil). The stimulus that produces a natural response is referred to as the *unconditioned stimulus* (US) because the animal does not need to learn what to do in response to that stimulus. The US produces a natural response. The stimulus that does not produce a response is referred to as the *conditioned stimulus* (CS) since the animal has to learn, or become conditioned to, a response to this stimulus. If the animal can respond to classical conditioning, it will learn to associate the CS with the natural response.

In the 19th century, Russian scientist Ivan Pavlov conducted experiments where he trained his dogs to associate a bell ringing with feeding time, and therefore start to salivate. These famous experiments were examples of classical conditioning.

Electrophoresis Chamber
Build a scientific apparatus like the ones scientists use to analyze DNA.

This is what you'll need:

A plastic ice cube tray
A measuring cup
Water
A large microwave-safe bowl
1 teaspoon agar (available in
    health food stores)
1 teaspoon baking soda
Scissors
Aluminum foil

A butter knife
An eyedropper
Food coloring in four
    different colors
Connecting wires with
    alligator clips
A 9-volt battery

Here's what to do:

1. Wash the plastic ice cube tray thoroughly and let it dry.
2. Measure out ½ cup water and pour it into the large microwave-safe bowl.
3. Add the agar to the bowl and mix.
4. Microwave the water and agar for 15 seconds at a time, until the mixture just starts to boil. At that point, carefully take the bowl out of the microwave and set it aside for a few minutes.
5. While the agar is cooling, measure out ½ cup water. Add the baking soda to the water and mix to make the buffer solution. Set this aside.
6. Pour the slightly cooled agar into four wells in the ice cube tray. Do not overfill the wells—half full is more than enough. You need to make sure there is room for the buffer solution in each well.
7. Set the ice cube tray aside until the agar has completely cooled and hardened.
8. Cut eight 2-inch-wide strips of aluminum foil. Fold each strip over on itself (see the illustration below), so you are left with a thicker piece of foil that is 2 inches long and ½ inch wide. These will be the electrodes.

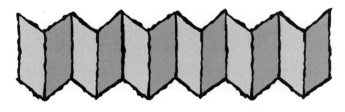

Fold the aluminum foil strip over on itself

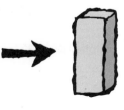

One thick piece
for the electrode

9. When the agar has hardened, use a butter knife as a cutting tool to cut a thin slit in the center of each block of agar.
10. Push one aluminum-foil electrode on either end of each block of agar, close to the edges.
11. Pour some buffer solution over one block of agar, filling the well completely. The agar block should be immersed in buffer solution. (See below.)

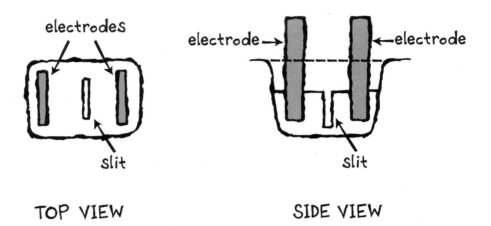

TOP VIEW   SIDE VIEW

12. Fill the eyedropper with the first food coloring. Carefully push the tip of the eyedropper down into the slit in the agar and then slowly release the color. Do not release it too quickly.
13. When the slit is filled with color, remove the eyedropper carefully so you don't disturb the color.
14. Use the alligator clips to connect the positive terminal of the 9-volt battery to one aluminum foil electrode and the negative terminal to the other electrode.
15. Observe what happens to the food coloring after one hour. Record your observations.
16. Continue watching the food coloring for two more hours, making observations every 30 minutes. Record what you notice the color doing.
17. Repeat this experiment with the other three food colorings. Record any differences between what you see using different colors.

What you should notice:

◆ The color spreads in only one direction.
◆ The food coloring may split into several different bands of color that move at different speeds through the agar.

Here's what's happening:

The process demonstrated by this experiment is called *electrophoresis*. When the aluminum foil electrodes are connected to the battery, a current runs through the buffer solution, creating an electric field through the agar block. The agar, even when it has hardened, has many small holes in it—it is considered porous. Because of the surrounding electric field, electrically charged molecules can pass through these holes, but they move at different speeds depending on their sizes. Small molecules move quickly through the agar; larger molecules move more slowly.

The food coloring you used in this experiment is made from mixtures of different molecules. When they are run through the electrophoresis chamber, the different molecules separate into bands of color. Also, the molecules are different in size, so some bands consisting of smaller molecules move faster and travel farther in the same amount of time it takes other bands of larger molecules to move a smaller distance.

The bands of color also only run toward one electrode. This is because the molecules in the food coloring become charged in the buffer solution. They are attracted to the electrode of the opposite charge and repelled from the electrode of the same charge. Having all the molecules in the sample run in the same direction allows them to be effectively separated by size in this electrophoresis method.

Dig a little deeper:

In "Spinach DNA" on page 33, you learned that DNA is a charged molecule. Since it is charged, scientists can use electrophoresis to separate different fragments of DNA according to size. This is very useful, especially for things like genetic tests. By comparing a given person's pattern of DNA bands against the known pattern for a disease, scientists can tell if that person is at risk for that disease. Gel electrophoresis can also be used in paternity tests. By comparing a child's pattern of DNA to his or her parents', scientists can figure out how people are related.

Things to try:

→ Make a new sample by mixing two colors of food coloring. Run this sample through the electrophoresis chamber. Compare the pattern of bands this produces to the pattern of bands produced when a single-colored sample is used. How does this test compare to DNA testing for paternity?

→ Fill the slit of one agar block with food coloring, but do not connect the electrodes to the battery. What happens to the color? Does it still spread? What does this prove about the pores in the agar?

Digestive Enzymes
Learn how these molecular scissors make a big difference.

This is what you'll need:

A pancreatin capsule (available from a health
  food store or drugstore)
A ziplock bag
A rolling pin (or something heavy to help
  crush the pancreatin capsule)
Plastic disposable cups
Water
A casserole dish
Ice cubes
Unflavored gelatin
A large bowl
Measuring spoons
A marker

Here's what to do:

1. Seal one pancreatin capsule inside the ziplock bag. Place the bag on a counter and use the rolling pin to crush the pill into a powder to make it easier to dissolve.
2. Pour the pancreatin powder into a disposable cup. Add 3 tablespoons of water. Mix well.
3. Fill the casserole dish with ice cubes. Mix the unflavored gelatin with water in the large bowl according to package instructions.
4. Quickly pour some liquid gelatin into two disposable cups.
5. Add 1 tablespoon of the pancreatin solution to one of the cups and label this cup with your marker.
6. Place both cups of gelatin in the casserole dish.
7. After 30 minutes, take the cups out of the casserole dish and swirl them around. Record any changes in texture you notice.

What you should notice:

◆ The gelatin cup where pancreatin solution was not added hardened in 30 minutes.

◆ The gelatin cup where pancreatin solution was added stayed liquid.

Here's what's happening:

If you read the nutritional information on the gelatin package, you'll see that a large component of gelatin is protein. In your stomach, proteins are broken down and digested by enzymes. Enzymes are proteins that help speed up chemical reactions. The pancreatin capsules contain some of these digestive enzymes. If your stomach didn't contain digestive enzymes, your body would not be able to get the nutrients it needs from the food you eat.

For gelatin to harden, the proteins in it take on a specific structure. When the proteins are broken down, however, the gelatin can no longer arrange itself in the correct way. When you added the pancreatin solution to one of the cups of gelatin, the solution contained an enzyme called *trypsin*. Trypsin cuts up and chemically "digests" the proteins in the gelatin, meaning that gelatin solution never hardens.

Dig a little deeper:

You can think of digestive enzymes as molecular scissors that cut up long proteins. All digestive enzymes, however, do not break down proteins in the same way. Many require very specific configurations of amino acids (the building blocks of proteins) to be able to find a spot to cut. Trypsin is a more active "cutter" since fewer conditions need to be met for trypsin to snip away at proteins.

Things to try:

➜ What happens if you add some pancreatin solution to gelatin that has already hardened? Does the gelatin break down? Why or why not?

Making a Mummy

For the ancient Egyptians, mummifying their dead relatives was a part of their religious duties. In this experiment, you can make your own mummy, using a fish instead of, well, your mommy.

This is what you'll need:

A small fish that has been scaled and gutted

A measuring tape

A kitchen scale

2 1-pound boxes baking soda

A plastic container large enough to totally submerge the fish

Safety Warning: **Always** *remember to wash your hands thoroughly with soap after handling raw meat.* **Also** *remember never to use live fish for this experiment!*

Here's what to do:

1. Measure the fish head to tail and weigh it on the kitchen scale. Record these measurements, as well as the general appearance of the fish. (Is the skin shiny or dull? What color is the fish? What does it smell like?)
2. Pour a 1- or 2-inch-thick layer of baking soda into the plastic container.
3. Pack the gut cavity of the fish with baking soda.
4. Place the fish on top of the layer of baking soda in the plastic container.
5. Pour more baking soda into the container so the fish is totally buried in baking soda. There should be a 1- to 2-inch-thick layer of baking soda all around the fish.
6. Place the plastic container someplace it won't be disturbed.
7. After a week, take out the fish and record your observations. Clean the baking soda out of the gut cavity and weigh the fish. Record the weight.
8. Pack the fish in fresh baking soda and put it back in the container for another week.
9. Record your observations about the fish's appearance, weight, and length after a total of two weeks in baking soda.

What you should notice:

◆ After a week in baking soda, the fish will weigh less and feel rougher.
◆ After two weeks in baking soda, the fish will have lost around half its body weight and feel leathery.

Here's what's happening:

The baking soda you use in this experiment does one very important thing for the fish mummy—it absorbs water. If you examine the baking soda that was closest to the fish in the plastic container, you may notice that it feels a bit moist. The baking soda was used to dehydrate the fish's body. Removing water from the tissues and cells of the fish helps to preserve, or mummify, the body.

All living things, including bacteria and fungi, require water to live. A dead fish left out exposed to air without being dehydrated would soon decay. Microorganisms would grow on the dead tissue, creating a strong, unpleasant odor. By dehydrating the fish, the growth of bacteria and fungi is slowed down because with less water available, fewer microorganisms can grow.

Dig a little deeper:

The ancient Egyptians used a naturally occurring chemical to mummify their dead. This chemical was called *natron*, and it was found on the banks of the Nile. Natron is actually a salt consisting primarily of sodium carbonate. Other components of natron include sodium sulfate, sodium chloride, and about 17 percent sodium bicarbonate.

Sodium bicarbonate is commonly known now as baking soda. The chemical structure of baking soda molecules is special. When many baking soda molecules mass together, they arrange themselves in such a way that there is room for water molecules to fit into the arrangement. The baking soda doesn't dissolve into the water; instead, a certain amount of water can be absorbed into the baking soda. This process is known as *desiccation*; baking soda is therefore considered a *desiccant*. Desiccants are used every day to keep moisture out. For example, you know those little packets that come with new shoes? Those packets contain a dessicant called silica gel, which keeps the shoes moisture-free.

Goldfish, Cold Fish
The level of an animal's activity is affected by temperature.

This is what you'll need:

- A small jar
- Water
- A goldfish
- A thermometer
- A stopwatch
- A large bowl, deep enough to hold at least half of the jar
- Ice cubes
- A thermometer
- *Safety Warning: Since you are working with a live animal, use care to prevent hurting it.*

Here's what to do:

1. Transfer the goldfish into the jar and add enough water to make him comfortable.
2. Use the thermometer to record the temperature of the water.
3. Use the stopwatch to time 30 seconds, and count how many times the goldfish opens and closes his mouth in that time. Record the number.
4. Place the jar inside the bowl. Fill the bowl with cold water and some ice cubes. *Do not* put ice cubes directly into the jar with the goldfish.
5. After five minutes, use the thermometer to record the temperature of the water.
6. Use the stopwatch to time 30 seconds again, and count how many times the goldfish opens and closes his mouth in that time. Record the number.

What you should notice:

◆ The goldfish moves his mouth less frequently in colder water.

Here's what's happening:

All animals, including goldfish, use energy when they move. They also need energy for basic life processes, to keep their hearts beating, and for digestion. The rate at which an animal uses energy for all the things it needs to do is called the *metabolic rate*. Metabolic rates can change with activity; for example, when you play basketball, your metabolic rate is higher than when you are sleeping.

Goldfish are different from humans and other mammals in how their metabolic rate is regulated. Mammals are *homeotherms*, or warm-blooded. Their body temperature is not dependent on outside temperatures because mammals regulate their temperature using metabolic rates. Goldfish are *ectotherms*, which means their body temperature depends on the temperature of their surroundings, and their metabolic rates rise or fall depending on how hot or cold it is.

When the goldfish's surroundings get colder, its body automatically begins to save energy, and its rate of metabolism goes down. One way to save energy is to not move as much. That is why the number of times the goldfish's mouth moves decreases in colder water. Its metabolic rate drops and it uses less oxygen.

Dig a little deeper:

When environmental factors result in reduced activity for an animal, the animal goes into *torpor*. Goldfish go into torpor when temperatures are reduced, as you saw in this experiment. Since their metabolic rate decreases, their activity level decreases as well, and the goldfish requires much less food.

Interestingly, the metabolic rate of some animals drops so significantly in cold temperatures that they can survive being almost completely frozen. For example, an alligator can survive being frozen in a lake for weeks as long as his nose is free to breathe—in alligators, the metabolic rate is reduced to the point that in such cold temperatures, they don't even need to eat to survive!

Snail Salads
Explore the relationship between snails and algae.

This is what you'll need:

3 glass jars with lids
Pond water
3 microscope slides
Markers
Plastic wrap
6 aquarium snails (can be purchased from a pet store)
A magnifying glass
Safety Warning: Since you are working with live animals,
use care to prevent hurting them.

Here's what to do:

1. Wash, rinse, and dry the jars well, making sure there is no soap left on them.
2. Collect pond water in one of the jars.
3. Place all three microscope slides inside the pond water jar, making sure they do not touch each other. Prop them up against the sides of the jar so you can see them clearly without having to reach into the jar to touch them.
4. Replace the lid on the pond water jar and place the jar in direct sunlight. Observe the slides for a week. Record any changes you notice in the appearance of the slides.
5. After a week, fill the other two jars with fresh water and label one "Snails" and the other "No Snails."
6. Carefully remove all three microscope slides from the pond water jar. Place one slide gently on the plastic wrap. Place the other two slides in the new jars, one in each jar.
7. To the jar labeled "Snails," add the six aquarium snails. Replace the lids on the "Snails" and "No Snails" jars and place them in direct sunlight.
8. Observe the jars for two weeks, recording changes in the appearance of the slides, the number of snails, and the overall appearance of the water.

What you should notice:

◆ A thin film of algae grows on the surfaces of the microscope slides immersed in pond water. Under high magnification, you may be able to discern individual algae units.

◆ In the jar with no snails, the algae introduced on the microscope slide will continue to grow. The water in that jar will become cloudy and green over time. In the jar with snails, the snails will feed on the algae. Algae growth will be slower because the snails graze on it.

Here's what's happening:

In "Algae Farming" on page 42, you learned that algae actually consists of tiny plants that grow in pond water. These plants tend to stick to surfaces like glass, which is why you were able to see a thin film on the microscope slides.

The little bit of algae on the film on a microscope slide, when transferred into a new jar of fresh water, is able to continue growing until the water gets cloudy and green from excess algae growth. In the jar with the snails, however, you probably noticed the algae grew more slowly. The snails grazed on the algae as they crept inside the jar, reducing the overall amount of algae.

If you were to leave the snails and algae in the jar over a long period of time, you would notice that the amount of algae and the population of snails would fluctuate for a while. Some of the time, it might look as if the snails are eating a lot of the algae while they grow and reproduce rapidly. At another point, if the amount of algae gets very low, some of the snails may die out, which then leads to an overgrowth of algae. Eventually, the snails and the algae would reach some sort of balance within the ecosystem of the jar, where the snail population is not so large that it eats up too much algae, and the amount of algae is enough to feed the snails. This point of balance is called *equilibrium*.

Dig a little deeper:

Even though algae is a normal part of the environment, in some places, it can grow out of control and cause damage to the surroundings. In the Mediterranean, a species of algae is spreading unchecked and creating problems for the rest of the ecosystem. A type of shell-less snail from Florida is being introduced to eat the overgrown algae to prevent further damage.

MORE THAN MEETS THE EYE

Spores and More
Take a closer look at ferns.

This is what you'll need:

Water
Microscope slides and cover slips
A fern plant (or some intact fern leaves)
Tweezers
Rubbing alcohol
A microscope
Safety Warning: Be careful when handling chemicals like rubbing alcohol, since direct contact can be harmful.

Here's what to do:

1. Place a drop of water on a slide.
2. With tweezers, scrape some small, dark spore casings (called *sporangia*) from the leaves. Sporangia may be found under the leaf or tucked into the leaf of the fern. If you have a hard time finding the sporangia, cut a leaf off the fern plant and place it in a plastic bag. After a day or two, remove the leaf and shake the small, dark sporangia out of the bottom of the bag and onto a microscope slide.
3. Carefully place a cover slip over the sporangia and examine them under the microscope. Make sketches of what you see.
4. Prepare another slide of sporangia in the same way as before, but use alcohol instead of water.
5. Carefully place a cover slip over this slide and examine it under the microscope. Make sketches of what you see, noting any differences between this slide and the previous slide.

What you should notice:

◆ When the sporangia are exposed to alcohol, they burst open and release spores.

Here's what's happening:

The spores are held inside the saclike sporangia, which are the reproductive organs of the fern. The spores are essentially the seeds of the fern, and each one is a single cell. When conditions are right for the fern to release its spores, the sporangia burst open and the spores fall to the ground. Very few spores actually grow into new ferns; millions die every season.

In nature, the sporangia release spores when they are dehydrated, or dried. When mounted on a slide with water, the sporangia stay intact. In this experiment, exposing the sporangia to alcohol effectively dehydrates them. This is why the spores were released.

Dig a little deeper:

Compare the single-celled spores to other cells you've examined. (See "Cell Staining" on page 30.) What differences do you notice? Can you identify any similar cell structures?

Yeast Babies
Examine how yeast are "born."

This is what you'll need:

1 cup warm water
1 package active dry yeast
1 tablespoon sugar
A bowl
Methylene blue (available at aquarium
    supply stores)
An eyedropper
Microscope slides and cover slips
A microscope

Safety Warning: Be careful when handling chemicals like methylene blue, since direct contact can be harmful.

Here's what to do:

1. Mix the water, active dry yeast, and sugar in the bowl.
2. Set the mixture aside for one hour.
3. After an hour, add 10 drops of methylene blue to the bowl.
4. Place a drop of the mixture on a microscope slide.
5. Carefully cover the liquid with a cover slip, making sure there are few or no bubbles of trapped air.
6. Examine the yeast cells under different magnifications on the microscope. Make note of differences in cell sizes.

What you should notice:

◆ Most of the yeast cells are uniform in size.
◆ Sometimes you will spot a smaller yeast cell, often attached to a larger cell.

Here's what's happening:

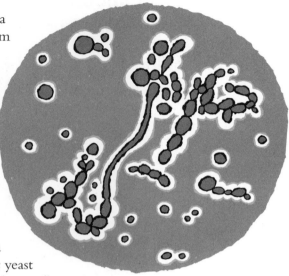

Most types of yeast cells reproduce in a process known as *budding*. This is a form of *asexual reproduction*, since only one parent is required to create offspring. In this type of reproduction, a single yeast cell can pinch off a new cell. The original yeast cell is called the *mother cell*; the newly formed cell that buds off from the mother is called the *daughter cell*.

In a mixture of growing and reproducing yeast cells, as you have here, you may be able to see evidence of budding. Sometimes, there will be a larger yeast cell connected to a smaller yeast cell—the large cell is the mother and the small one is the daughter.

Things to try:

→ Prepare a culture of yeast cells without the sugar and examine it. Do you see any evidence of budding without the presence of sugar? Why or why not? What does this prove about yeast cells' need for nutrients in order to grow?

Yeast Balloons
Blow up a balloon with a little yeast.

This is what you'll need:

- 2 small, empty plastic soda bottles
- 2 cups warm water
- 3 tablespoons sugar
- 2 packages active dry yeast
- 2 latex balloons
- Tape

Here's what to do:

1. Rinse out the soda bottles.
2. Pour 1 cup of fairly warm water into each bottle.
3. Add all the sugar to one bottle of water and mix. *Do not* add sugar to the other bottle.
4. Pour the contents of one package of yeast into each bottle. Swirl the mixture around to mix.
5. Attach a balloon over the mouth of each bottle. You can add some tape around the edges to secure the balloons in place.
6. Observe what happens to the balloons after 5 minutes, 15 minutes, and 30 minutes. Record your observations.

What you should notice:

◆ Over time, the balloon on the bottle that had sugar in it should inflate quite a bit.
◆ On the bottle that didn't have sugar in it, the balloon may inflate a little bit, but not nearly to the extent that the other balloon inflates.

Here's what's happening:

A package of active dry yeast actually contains living yeast cells. Yeast cells, like any other living organisms, need to change food into energy in order to do the things they need to do to survive. In this experiment, the food source is the sugar. The yeast cells use oxygen from the air and the sugar in the solution to produce carbon dioxide, water, and energy. This process is called *aerobic respiration*, which is the same process that the cells in the human body use to produce energy.

Even when there is no oxygen available, yeast cells are able to make energy through a process called *anaerobic respiration*, where the sugar is used to produce carbon dioxide, alcohol, and energy. Compared to aerobic respiration, anaerobic respiration produces far less energy. In addition, the alcohol produced during anaerobic respiration is toxic to the yeast. If the yeast cells are forced to use anaerobic respiration for energy, eventually they will all die.

In this experiment, covering the bottle with a balloon cuts off the oxygen supply to the yeast. Until the trapped oxygen runs out, the cells use aerobic respiration to produce energy. When they've used up all the oxygen, however, they have to switch to anaerobic respiration. The by-product of this process, the carbon dioxide, is what inflates the balloon. (Since carbon dioxide is a by-product of aerobic respiration as well, the balloon will begin inflating even before the oxygen runs out. Since carbon dioxide continues to be produced and the balloon continues to inflate, this experiment proves that yeast cells are able to respirate anaerobically.)

Neither form of respiration will take place without a food source—in this case, the sugar. That's why the balloon over the bottle with yeast but no sugar does not inflate; those yeast cells are not respiring.

Dig a little deeper:

Since anaerobic respiration can produce toxic by-products, cells prefer aerobic respiration. However, in the absence of oxygen, anaerobic respiration is better than the alternative—dying. The cells in your body sometimes undergo anaerobic respiration. When you have exercised too hard and your muscles cramp, what is happening is that your muscle cells are producing energy through anaerobic respiration, which produces lactic acid. The lactic acid gives you the cramp.

Things to try:

→ Determine if temperature has an effect on the speed of anaerobic respiration by using different water samples of various temperatures.

→ Since you know that anaerobic respiration produces by-products that are toxic to yeast, leave this experiment running for a few days. Does the balloon stop inflating at some point? Does this mean the yeast cells are dead, or that the sugar has run out? Add some more sugar to the bottle and replace the balloon. Does the balloon start inflating again?

How Clean Are Your Hands?

Make special microbes by culturing plates to see what is growing on your hands.

This is what you'll need:

An adult to help with all the "cooking" steps
An oven
1 14.5-ounce can chicken broth
A saucepan
3 teaspoons agar (available in health
    food stores)
An oven-safe bowl
A casserole dish large enough to hold the
    bowl with room around the edges
Oven mitts
A dozen small plastic disposable plates, preferably
    clear, deep enough to hold a thin layer of liquid
Aluminum foil
A kitchen thermometer
Tape and a marker
Safety Warning: Have an adult supervise when using the stove.

Here's what to do:

1.   Make nutrient agar plates to grow bacterial cultures:

1A. Preheat your oven to 300°F.

1B. Pour the broth into the saucepan and add the agar. Mix it well.

1C. At this point, it may be best to have an adult take over, unless you have experience working with stoves and ovens.

1D. Slowly heat the mixture on the stovetop, stirring the whole time, until the agar has completely dissolved.

1E. When the agar has dissolved, pour the liquid into the oven-safe bowl (if the saucepan is oven-safe, you can leave the liquid in the saucepan).

1F. Place the bowl in the casserole dish, and put everything into the oven. (The casserole dish is to catch any spills if the agar mixture bubbles over.)

1G. Heat the mixture in the oven for 20 minutes.

1H. Use the oven mitts to carefully remove the bowl and casserole dish from the oven. Set everything aside to cool slightly. Don't wait too long. You don't want the agar mixture to harden, but the mixture should be less than 300° when you pour it.

II. Lay the clear plastic plates out on a countertop. Arrange them so you can easily pour the agar mixture into them.

IJ. When the mixture has cooled but is still liquid, pour a thin layer into each plate. Cover the plates with aluminum foil (be careful not to spill any liquid) and set them aside for one hour.

IK. You can make extra plates and store them, covered, in the refrigerator. These plates will probably be good for two or three days. Although you should make sure everything is clean to reduce the amount of bacteria on your plates before the experiment, because you aren't sterilizing the equipment, the plates will grow fuzzy in a few days.

2. Press your finger lightly on the surface of one plate.

3. Have friends and family members press their fingers on the surface of some plates as well.

4. Leave one plate untouched.

5. Re-cover all the plates with aluminum foil. Attach tape labels that mark which plate belongs to whom.

6. Place the plates somewhere they won't be disturbed for two days.

7. After two days, take the foil off and examine the plates. Record any growth you see (make notes of texture, color, etc.).

What you should notice:

◆ Compared with the plate that was not touched, there should more growth (measured in terms of fuzzy, slimy, or slick patches) on the plates that came into contact with fingers. Different people's plates may look different.

Here's what's happening:

No matter how much you wash, your hands are covered with microorganisms, or microbes. In fact, your whole body is covered with microbes. Usually, the microbes do not harm you; sometimes they can be helpful. These microbes need a food source for energy. Usually, they can feed on other things on your skin, but you can also grow them in a special type of dish used in laboratories. The nutrient agar plates you made are similar to the type of dishes scientists use to study microbes.

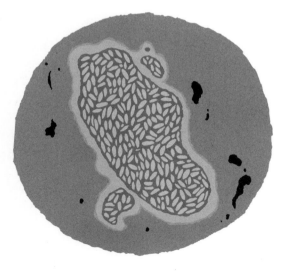

In this experiment, you made sure everything was clean, but you didn't sterilize your materials. Sterilization requires conditions that are hard to achieve at home. In a laboratory, scientists would sterilize their equipment in an autoclave (a special kind of steam oven). Because your equipment wasn't sterile, some microbes will always be present.

This experiment does, however, give you an idea of how many microbes are present on your skin by comparing the growth of microbes on the plate you touched versus the plate that was not touched. Now that you know what's really on your hands, make sure you listen when your parents tell you to wash up before dinner!

Things to try:

→ Press your finger onto one nutrient agar plate, wash your hands with soap, then press your clean finger onto another nutrient agar plate. Let the plates grow for two days. What differences do you notice between the two plates? Are there still bacteria on your hands even after you wash them?

Making Yogurt

Yogurt is made by growing bacteria with a fairly simple process you can do at home.

This is what you'll need:

A measuring cup
Water
A marker
Plastic cups
Whole milk
A saucepan
A kitchen thermometer
Plain yogurt from the grocery store (check the
    label to make sure it says "active culture")
Powdered milk
Aluminum foil
A cooler
4 small plastic soda bottles
3 cups hot water
Safety Warning: Have an adult supervise when using the stove.

Here's what to do:

1. Using the measuring cup, pour 1 cup of water into a plastic cup and mark the level of the liquid with the marker. Repeat so you have three plastic cups marked at the 1-cup mark.

2. Heat 3 cups of milk in a saucepan on the stovetop until the milk reaches a temperature of 175°F. Check the temperature using the kitchen thermometer. (Have an adult help you with this step since you'll be working with very hot liquids.)

3. Let the milk cool until it is 120°F so that it is easier to work with.

4. Pour the milk into each of the three plastic cups, stopping at the marker lines.

5. Microwave a few tablespoons of yogurt for 10 seconds to heat it up.

6. Label one cup "Milk Only" and set it aside.

7. Label another cup "Milk and Yogurt." Add 1 tablespoon of yogurt to this cup and mix well. Set it aside.

8. Label the last cup "Milk, Powdered Milk, and Yogurt." Add 1 tablespoon of powdered milk and 1 tablespoon of yogurt to this cup and mix well. Set it aside.

9. Cover all three cups with aluminum foil and place them inside the cooler.

10. Fill the four plastic soda bottles with very hot water and seal them tight. Place these inside the cooler as well.

11. Use the thermometer to monitor the temperature of the cooler, which needs to stay at about 110°F for the entire time you culture the yogurt. If it starts to cool down, refill the water bottles with hot water.

12. After six hours, check on the cups. Record any changes in appearance, texture, and odor.

13. After 12 hours (or overnight), check on the cups. Record any changes in appearance, texture, and odor.

What you should notice:

◆ The cup labeled "Milk Only" will look and smell more and more like rotten milk as time passes.

◆ The cups labeled "Milk and Yogurt" and "Milk, Powdered Milk, and Yogurt" won't look or smell rotten; instead, they will appear yogurt-y.

◆ The cup labeled "Milk, Powdered Milk, and Yogurt" will have a thicker consistency, more like yogurt, than the cup labeled "Milk and Yogurt."

Here's what's happening:

Believe it or not, yogurt is made by adding special bacteria to milk and letting the bacteria grow until the milk appears yogurt-y. The bacteria feed on the lactose in the milk (lactose is a type of sugar). When the bacteria break the lactose down, they make lactic acid, which is responsible for giving yogurt its distinctive sour taste. The process of changing the lactose into lactic acid also thickens the milk.

Live yogurt cultures can be found in almost any yogurt in the grocery store, so long as the package says "active cultures." These cultures can be used to make yogurt at home, although you have to be careful about monitoring the conditions. If the temperatures are not correct, the yogurt may have too much bacteria in it or the milk may rot before the yogurt is made. This is why you shouldn't eat the yogurt you made in this experiment.

Things to try:

→ Try using starter cultures from flavored yogurts or different brands of yogurt. Does this make a difference?

→ Try using milk substitutes (heavy cream, infant formula) instead of milk. How does this affect the yogurt-making process?

→ What happens if you use lactose-free milk in this experiment?

There's Fungus among Us

You can grow a colorful garden of mold with a clear jar and some old food.

This is what you'll need:

A large, clear jar (like an old mayonnaise or jelly jar) with a lid
Leftover food (Anything from your refrigerator would work,
  but fresh foods like fruits, vegetables, or cheeses would be best.
  Try to avoid prepackaged foods like packaged cakes or cookies.
  Do not use meat or fish—the smell would be unbearable!)
Water
Tape

Here's what to do:

1. Place the jar on its side on a table.
2. Gather five or six types of food and make sure it all fits inside the jar without overcrowding.
3. Dip each piece of food in some water and put everything back inside the jar.
4. Screw on the lid and seal it with tape. Label the jar with the words "Fungus Garden" so that everyone will know what it is. (After you've grown your fungus garden, you will have to throw everything—including the jar—away. Do not reopen the jar, because mold is not a good thing for people to smell or breathe.)
5. Place the jar in a place it will not be knocked over or disturbed.
6. Record any changes in the food every day for two weeks.

What you should notice:

◆ After three or four days, you should start to see fuzzy mold growing on some of the food.

◆ Over the course of two weeks, you may notice many different types of molds growing. For example, there may be different colors (blue, green, white) or different textures (fuzzy, bumpy, flat).

◆ You may notice mold spreading from one food to another. Keep a record of how many different kinds of mold you can identify inside the jar, as well as how many different types of mold you can identify on a single piece of food.

Here's what's happening:

Unlike plants that grow from seeds, molds (which are a type of fungus) grow from tiny spores that float in the air. Most of the food you eat, even fresh food, is covered in many of these tiny spores. Mold cannot make its own food. Instead it feeds on the stuff it grows on. Molds produce chemicals that cause food to rot and then take nutrients from the rotting materials.

There are many different kinds of mold, as you probably noticed if you used many different kinds of food in your mold garden. Though molds can be disgusting, they can be useful too. When things rot in a forest, for example, they return nutrients to the soil. Since molds help speed up the rotting process, they are important in the process of "recycling" nutrients. Also, people have been able to extract different chemicals from molds that help treat human diseases. Alexander Fleming extracted penicillin, a drug that treats bacterial infections, from a mold growing in his laboratory.

Dig a little deeper:

Molds are a type of fungus that is generally not eaten. Mushrooms, on the other hand, are fungi as well, and many mushrooms are completely edible and even yummy! Of course, if you see wild mushrooms growing in your yard or in a park, don't eat them, because you can't be sure if they are a safe fungus or not.

Though most moldy food should be thrown away, some foods are actually tastier with mold! For example, blue cheese gets its name and its distinctive flavor from the bluish-colored mold that grows in the cracks of the cheese. In fact, when wheels of blue cheese are made, people poke holes through the cheese to give the mold a place to grow as the cheese ripens.

Things to try:

→ Some foods, especially prepackaged foods, contain preservatives to prevent them from decaying quickly. You can test to see how effective these preservatives are by using two new fungus gardens. Set up one garden with a piece of packaged cake and another with a piece of freshly baked cake. Which one grows fungus first?

→ Some chemicals around the house, like table salt or baking soda, are natural preservatives. Test how effective these preservatives are by using two new fungus gardens. Set up one garden with an apple and a piece of bread, and another with the same foods as well as 3 or 4 tablespoons of baking soda. Which one grows fungus first?

The Science of Soap
Are all soaps equal in the eyes of a germ?

This is what you'll need:

A marker

Disposable cups

Water

Disgusting mud sample

4 different kinds of soap (Make sure one sample is an antibacterial
cleanser; the others can be hand soap, dishwashing detergent,
laundry detergent, bath soap, or scented body wash. You can
try as many samples as you want, as long as you have enough
plates for all the samples.)

Cotton swabs

6 nutrient agar plates from "How Clean Are Your Hands?" (see page 64)

Masking tape

Aluminum foil

Here's what to do:

1. Label six disposable cups as follows: (cup 1) Water [negative control];
   (cup 2) Water + Mud [positive control]; (cup 3) Water + Mud + Soap #1;
   (cup 4) Water + Mud + Soap #2; (cup 5) Water + Mud + Soap #3;
   (cup 6) Water + Mud + Soap #4.

2. Fill each cup with 1 cup of water.

3. Add ⅛ teaspoon of the mud to each cup that has "Mud" on the label (don't
   put any mud in the cup labeled "Water [negative control]").

4. Add ¼ teaspoon of Soap #1, Soap #2, Soap #3, and Soap #4 to the
   corresponding cups. If any of your soaps are solids, you can use a cheese
   grater to grate them, and then add ¼ teaspoon of the shavings.

5. Using a different cotton swab for each cup, mix the contents of the cups
   well.

6. Place a nutrient agar plate in front of each cup. To keep track of the plates,
   you can label a small piece of masking tape that can later be attached to the
   foil cover of the plate.

7. Using the cotton swabs, swab some liquid from each cup onto the plates.

8. Cover all the plates with aluminum foil. Attach the tape labels if necessary.

9. Place the plates somewhere they won't be disturbed for two days.

10. After two days, take the foil off and examine the plates. Record any growths
    you see (make notes of texture, color, etc.).

What you should notice:

- There should be no growth—or very, very little growth—on the plate marked "Water [negative control]."
- There should be a good amount of growth on the plate marked "Mud [positive control]."
- There should be varying amounts of growth on the plates where you tested the different soaps.

Here's what's happening:

Everyone knows that mud is dirty—and now you know it's full of microbes as well. The plate that you added just mud to will become disgusting in a few days. All sorts of fuzzy and slimy bacteria and fungi will grow all over it. The plates treated with soap, however, will have varying amounts of growth on them, depending on the type of soap you used.

Regular bath soap or hand soap, believe it or not, does not really kill germs. Instead, when you wash with these soaps, the microbes on your skin get lifted so they can be rinsed off more easily with water. Many of the household soaps you may have used in this experiment may not have been effective in reducing the amount of microbe growth on the nutrient agar plates.

If you used a sample of antibacterial soap, you probably noticed a dramatic difference in the amount of microbe growth on this plate compared to the others. Antibacterial soap is able to directly kill microbes, where other soaps cannot.

Dig a little deeper:

Even though antibacterial soaps are available on the market and they do effectively kill microbes, many scientists feel strongly that these should not be used in the home. Overusing antibacterial products can lead to some microbes becoming resistant to the antibiotics in the product. That means the antibacterial chemical will eventually become useless for killing microbes. The Centers for Disease Control and Prevention (CDC) has suggested that regular soap is fine for the general public, and antibacterial soaps should be saved for health care, child care, and food preparation settings where the accidental transfer of microbes can be especially harmful.

Things to try:

→ Try this experiment using household cleansers like bleach, window cleaner, or furniture polish. Do these kill microbes?

Column of Colorful Bacteria

You too can grow your own multicolored bacteria.

This is what you'll need:

Mud from an outdoor source like around a pond
(the smellier the mud, the more microorganisms
it is likely to contain)
1 egg
2 sheets of notebook paper, shredded
A clear plastic bottle with a cap
Funnel (optional; for pouring the mud into the bottle)
Water (pond water or other water from an outdoor source
is best, but not required)
A bowl and spoon for mixing
Safety Warning: At the end of this experiment, have an
adult properly dispose of the column.

Here's what to do:

1. Mix together the mud, egg, and shredded paper.
2. Pour the mud mixture into the bottle, filling it almost all the way. You can use the funnel to help you pour.
3. Pour water into the bottle slowly, making sure there is a small amount of unabsorbed water at the top. Again, you can use the funnel to make the pouring easier.
4. Loosely screw on the cap. The cap will help prevent a nasty mess if your bottle gets knocked over, but you don't want to seal the bottle off completely—as bacteria grow in the bottle, they will release gases. If the bottle cap is screwed on tight, the gas pressure can build until the bottle explodes! To make sure this doesn't happen, vent the bottle every few days by taking off the cap for a few minutes.
5. Place the bottle on a sunny windowsill.
6. Record what happens over the next three to four months, making observations at least once a week.

What you should notice:

◆ In a few weeks, you should be able to see different colors of bacteria growing at different levels of the Winogradsky column.

Here's what's happening:

The *Winogradsky column*, illustrated at the bottom of this page, is a sort of independent environment for bacteria. It demonstrates how different microbes need different conditions to survive. It also illustrates the amount of diversity within microorganisms.

All living things can be classified according to how they get energy. *Phototrophs* use light to make energy, and *chemotrophs* use chemical reactions. In addition, living things can be classified according to where they get carbon for different cellular processes. *Autotrophs* get their carbon from carbon dioxide gas, and *heterotrophs* get carbon from other organic compounds. From these descriptions, you may realize that plants are phototrophs and autotrophs (they use sunlight and carbon dioxide for respiration) and animals are chemotrophs and heterotrophs (they get carbon from the food they eat and make energy through chemical reactions). Bacteria are the only class of organism where all these categories are represented. Within a single Winogradsky column, you can find examples of each of these types of life.

Near the top of the column, sunlight and oxygen are abundant. In this zone, bacteria that use photosynthesis grow well. As you move lower down the column, oxygen levels diminish whereas sulfur levels increase. At the very bottom of the column, the bacteria do not use photosynthesis and instead use anaerobic respiration.

	Air	
Aerobic Zone	Water	Diatoms Cyanobacteria Protists
	Oxygen-dominated mud	Aerobic sulfur-oxidizing bacteria
Oxygen-Scarce Zone	Rust-Colored Zone	Purple non sulfur bacteria
	Red Zone	Purple sulfur bacteria
Anaerobic Zone	Green Zone	Green sulfur bacteria
	Anaerobic H_2S-Dominated Zone (black)	Sulfur-reducing bacteria

Dig a little deeper:

Compare the bacteria in your column to the Winogradsky column. How many zones can you identify?

Things to try:

→ With an adult's help, you can culture some of the bacteria from the Winogradsky column on nutrient agar plates (see "How Clean Are Your Hands?" on page 64 for instructions). Be careful that you don't spill any of the bacteria, as they can be harmful to your health. You can then place the bacteria on a glass slide and examine the samples under a microscope.

→ Make another column, but this time leave it in complete darkness, like in a closet. Do you see different bacteria growing?

Spontaneous Generation?

How did people prove that microorganisms do not appear spontaneously?

This is what you'll need:

2 glass jars with lids
Dishwashing detergent
Rubbing alcohol
Paper towels
1 can clear chicken broth
A pressure cooker

Safety Warning: Be careful when handling chemicals like rubbing alcohol, since direct contact can be harmful. Also, have an adult supervise when using the pressure cooker, as it can be very dangerous and difficult to use.

Here's what to do:

1. Wash both jars and one lid thoroughly with dishwashing detergent.
2. Rinse the inside of both jars and the lid with rubbing alcohol. Try not to touch the inside surfaces of the jars or lid. (Throughout this whole experiment, try not to touch anything directly with your hands or get them dirty in any way.) Let them drip-dry on paper towels.
3. While the jars dry, heat the chicken broth in a pressure cooker for 30 minutes.
4. After the broth has cooled down enough to handle and the jars have dried, pour roughly equal amounts of chicken broth into each jar.
5. Seal one jar with the lid; leave the other one open.
6. Set the jars aside out of direct sunlight someplace they won't be disturbed. Observe the jars once a day for a week. Record any changes in the broth over the week.

Here's what's happening:

For centuries, people believed that living things could appear spontaneously from nonliving things. For example, they noticed that frogs seemed to appear in the mud that was left after a river flooded, but when the soil dried, there were no frogs around. They concluded that muddy soil gave rise to frogs. Similarly, they noticed that mice seemed to appear when stored grain got moldy. They concluded that moldy grain gave rise to mice.

In 1668, an Italian physician named Francesco Redi did an experiment that showed that maggots did not come from rotting meat, as was previously thought. He placed a piece of rotting meat in an open container and another piece in a closed container. He showed that maggots only grew on the meat in the open container. Since he had also noticed flies buzzing around the open container of meat, he concluded that the maggots were coming from flies.

People still did not totally abandon the idea of spontaneous generation. Instead, they began to believe that "larger" organisms did not arise spontaneously, but microorganisms did. In the mid-1700s, a Scottish scientist named John Needham claimed that all inorganic matter had a "life force" that allowed microbes to grow. He demonstrated this by showing that soup exposed to air eventually grew bacteria and fungi. Needham even went so far as to briefly boil some soup, presumably to remove microbes already in it, and poured it into "clean" flasks sealed with cork. He still saw microbes growing, which he took as proof of his life force theory.

Twenty years later, an Italian biologist named Lazzaro Spallanzani tried to show that Needham was wrong. Spallanzani thought Needham's experiments were incomplete—that Needham did not boil the soup long enough to kill all the microbes, and that the cork seals were not airtight, which allowed microbes in the air to settle on the soup in the "clean" flasks. He made two batches of soup—one that was boiled for a few minutes like Needham's, and another that was boiled for an hour. The soup boiled for an hour was poured into a flask that was melted shut so nothing new could get into the flask. Spallanzani found that this soup stayed sterile. The soup boiled for a few minutes then sealed in a flask with its mouth melted shut did not stay sterile—microbes grew in a few days. Spallanzani believed this proved that boiling for a few minutes was not enough to sterilize the soup. This meant Needham's experiments were flawed from the beginning. In addition, Spallanzani poured some of the soup that was boiled for an hour into another flask and then sealed it with cork as Needham did. He noticed that this batch grew microbes as well, suggesting that microbes could get into the soup through the cork.

This experiment is a shortened version of Spallanzani's experiment. The microbes that grow in the open jar of chicken stock do not materialize out of nowhere. If that was the case, there would be a lot of microbe growth in the closed jar as well. Instead, exposure to microbes from the air causes microbe growth in the open jar. In the closed jar, microbes will eventually grow since the conditions you are working under are not completely sterile. Pressure cooking the chicken stock and rinsing the jar with alcohol help to remove many of the microbes, but are not enough to maintain a completely sterile environment.

Things to try:

➔ Examine some of the chicken stock under a microscope to study the microbes further.

PERFECT PLANT PROJECTS

The Oxygen Is Leaf-ing
What is bubbling out of the leaf?

This is what you'll need:
- A glass jar
- Water
- A healthy, green leaf free of browning
- A magnifying glass

Here's what to do:
1. Fill the jar with water. Submerge the leaf completely.
2. Place the jar in direct sunlight for one hour.
3. After an hour, examine the submerged leaf with a magnifying glass.

What you should notice:
- ◆ There should be thousands of tiny bubbles on the surface of the leaf.

Here's what's happening:

To survive, the cells of a plant undergo a process called *photosynthesis*. The plant uses water, carbon dioxide, chlorophyll (the substance that gives the plant a green color), and sunlight to produce energy. A by-product of photosynthesis is oxygen.

The bubbles that appear on the leaf are oxygen bubbles, created when the cells undergo photosynthesis. Normally, the oxygen would be released into the air, but underwater, many of the bubbles get trapped on the leaf, leaving evidence of the cells' activities.

Dig a little deeper:

Plants, and even some bacteria, use photosynthesis to make sugar. Chemically, the reaction looks like this:

$$H_2O \quad + \quad CO_2 \quad + \text{ Sunlight} \longrightarrow C_6H_{12}O_2 + \quad O_2$$

Water + Carbon dioxide + Sunlight $\longrightarrow$ Sugar + Oxygen

The sugar must then be converted into energy by the cells using the process of cellular respiration.

Things to try:

➜ What if you leave the jar in total darkness instead of in direct sunlight? Do you still see bubbles?

Sweaty Plants
Explore transpiration.

This is what you'll need:

2 empty soda bottles
Water
Red food coloring
Modeling clay
A healthy leaf with a long stem
Masking tape
A magnifying glass

Here's what to do:

1. Fill one soda bottle with water and add 10 drops of red food coloring to it.
2. Mold the modeling clay around the stem of the leaf so that the stem can extend into the bottle of water while the modeling clay seals the bottle.
3. Push the clay plug into the mouth of the full bottle.
4. Carefully turn the other bottle upside down and position it over the leaf and the clay seal.
5. Use masking tape to hold the two bottles in place.
6. Place the complete setup in direct sunlight for one hour.
7. After an hour, use the magnifying glass to examine the upper bottle. Do you see any red water there?

What you should notice:

◆ Tiny drops of red water end up in the upper bottle.

Here's what's happening:

Plants lose water vapor through their leaves all the time. Special holes called *stomata* are distributed through the leaves and are used by the plant to get rid of extra water it may have taken in through its roots. The process of losing water through the stomata is known as *transpiration*.

Normally, you don't see transpiration because plants lose water vapor little bits at a time. In this experiment, you were able to "trap" the released water in the upper bottle. The red food coloring helped prove that the plant was using the water it took up through its stem for its cellular processes, including transpiration, and made it easier to see the water that had passed through the leaf.

Things to try:

➜ If you use a bigger leaf, does more water end up in the upper bottle?

Rainbow Flowers

Using a little bit of food coloring and water, you can change the color of a white flower—from the inside.

This is what you'll need:

- Some small paper cups
- Water
- Different food colorings
- Scissors
- White flowers (carnations work really well)

Here's what to do:

1. Partially fill the paper cups with water and then add a different food coloring to each cup.
2. Cut the stem of each flower so it is a little longer than the height of the paper cup. You might want an adult's help to cut the stems.
3. Place a flower in each paper cup.
4. Record how the flowers change over a 24-hour period.
5. After the first 24 hours, change the flowers around—for example, put the flower that used to be in the cup with red water into the cup with blue water. Put a flower that used to be in colored water into clear water. Record how the flowers change.

What you should notice:

◆ The flowers slowly change colors to match the color of the water.

Here's what's happening:

Just as humans have veins and arteries to transport fluids and nutrients, plants have a similar transport system. Structures called *xylem* and *phloem* carry food and water through the plant. The phloem is a specialized tube used to transport food; the xylem is used to transport water and minerals.

When a plant transpires and loses water from the stomata in the leaves, it has to replenish that water somehow. To do this, the plant sucks water up from its roots through the xylem. Small particles like food coloring can be sucked up through the plant along with the water—this is why the white carnations take on a color when they are placed in colored water. When the cells fill with water, they take up food coloring as well.

Dig a little deeper:

Transpiration is a continuous process, and the water inside a plant is always being cycled. This is the reason that a carnation dyed with food coloring can be "bleached" with clear water—over time, the colored water is lost through the stomata and clear water fills the cells again. As long as the carnation is alive and healthy, you can keep dyeing and bleaching it using alternating cups of colored and clear water.

Things to try:

→ Set up three paper cups with three different colors of water. Place a flower in the first cup, and then move it to another cup after three hours. Move it again every three hours. What happens to the colors of the petals?

→ Take a flower with a longer stem and use a knife to split the stem in half. Place one half of the stem in red water and the other half in blue water. What happens to the petals now?

Pinecone Plans
How do pinecones plan for the weather?

This is what you'll need:

A pinecone
A bucket of water

Here's what to do:

1. Examine the pinecone closely, noting the position of any seeds. Record your observations.
2. Submerge the pinecone in the bucket of water. Leave it submerged for one hour. Record any changes in its appearance every 15 minutes.
3. Remove the pinecone from the water and place it in a sunny spot. Predict how long it will take for the pinecone to return to the way it was before it was submerged in water.
4. Examine the pinecone every 30 minutes until it returns to its original condition.

What you should notice:

◆ When submerged in water, the scales of the pinecone close.
◆ It takes longer for the pinecone to reopen once it is out of the water than it took to close.

Here's what's happening:

Pine trees use pinecones to protect their seeds. The bracts, or scales, of the pinecone close around the seeds when weather conditions are too harsh for seed survival and open to release seeds when the conditions are right. When the weather is rainy and the ground is very damp, there is a good chance that the seeds will rot before they have a chance to sprout. Under these conditions, the scales of the pinecone close. You demonstrated this by submerging the pinecone in the bucket of water.

The reason that the pinecone takes longer to reopen than it took to close in the first place also has to do with protecting the seeds from excess moisture. By staying closed until the conditions dry up considerably, the pinecone makes sure the chances of the seeds rotting are minimized.

Things to try:

→ Dip half the pinecone in water and keep the other half dry. How does this affect the way the scales close?

Grow, Potato, Grow

If you examine a potato, you will see many small "eyes," or spuds.
The spuds are the reproductive organs of potatoes; a new potato plant
will grow from a spud. But how many spuds on one potato will grow?

This is what you'll need:

Potting soil
Many large paper cups or small planting pots
Some potatoes with spuds
A marker
A knife
Rubber bands

Here's what to do:

1. Put some potting soil into the paper cups.
2. Separate one potato with numerous spuds from the rest of the group. Count the spuds and record the number. Plant this potato in a paper cup and label the cup "Control." Cover the potato with more soil.
3. Use the knife to cut the remaining potatoes into many pieces (you might want an adult to help you with this step). Make sure each piece has only one spud. Select two of the larger potato pieces and plant them individually into two paper cups. Label these cups "Small Piece, One Spud." Cover the pieces with more soil.
4. Select two potato pieces that each have one spud, and use a rubber band to join them together. Plant the joined pieces in a paper cup and label it "Two Pieces, Joined." Cover the pieces with more soil.
5. Select two potato pieces that each have one spud, and plant them in a paper cup. Do not join the pieces with a rubber band, but plant them fairly close to each other. Label this cup "Two Pieces, Not Joined." Cover the pieces with more soil.
6. Water all your experiments regularly for three to four weeks. After that, dig up the potatoes and examine them. Record your observations.

What you should notice:

◆ In the "Control" cup with the whole potato, only one spud will grow into a plant.
◆ In the "Small Piece, One Spud" cup, the spud will grow into a plant.
◆ In the "Two Pieces, Joined" cup, only one spud will grow into a plant.

Here's what's happening:

Just like people, plants sometimes need their space, especially when they are trying to grow. To prevent other plants from crowding too close, they release special chemicals called *allelochemicals*. In potatoes, each spud releases allelochemicals to prevent other spuds from sprouting.

If each spud tries to prevent all the others from growing, how do potato plants ever grow? Basically, there is a spud race. At first, all the spuds are growing and releasing allelochemicals. The more a plant grows, the less susceptible it is to allelochemicals and the more allelochemicals it is able to produce. In a potato, the fastest-growing spud eventually blocks the other spuds' growth.

In this experiment, you proved that only one spud per potato grew, and you proved that one spud prevents the growth of any nearby spud, not just the ones on the same potato. This suggests that the allelochemicals made by potatoes are released into the soil or transferred through water rather than staying within the potato.

Dig a little deeper:

Potatoes are special plants. Instead of only growing from seeds, a new potato plant can grow from the spud on another potato. A potato planted in the ground is actually the underground stem of the new plant. The stem extends aboveground to produce leaves, and it extends underground to produce more tubers, which are the things that we harvest to eat.

Things to try:

→ Select one of the potato pieces that has sprouted and join it to a new potato piece that has an eye. (Use a rubber band to ensure that they touch each other, but be careful not to damage the growing plant.) Plant them joined in a paper cup. Does the second potato piece sprout?

→ Select two of the potato pieces that have sprouted and join them together with a rubber band. Replant them in a paper cup. Do both plants continue to grow?

→ Select one of the potato pieces that has sprouted and destroy the sprout. Cut it off about an inch from the potato. Using a rubber band, join it to a new potato piece that has an eye. Plant them joined in a paper cup. Which of the potato pieces grows?

→ Select one of the potato pieces that has sprouted and destroy the sprout from the base. Cut it off as close to the potato as possible, removing any visible part of the original spud. Using a rubber band, join it to a new potato piece that has an eye. Plant them joined in a paper cup. Does the second potato piece grow?

Irresistible Force
What forces do plants follow?

This is what you'll need:

A small bowl
Water
12 kidney beans
Aluminum foil
Paper towels
A marker

Tape
An old record
A turntable (or record player)

Here's what to do:

1. Fill the bowl with water and submerge the kidney beans.
2. Let the beans soak in the water overnight in the refrigerator.
3. The next day, cut four 12-inch by 12-inch squares of aluminum foil. In the center of each square, place a paper towel that has been folded into a 4-inch square.
4. Moisten the paper towels and place three kidney beans on each square.
5. Fold the foil around the paper towels and beans to cover the beans completely.
6. Use the marker to label each packet. Write "Center" on one edge of each packet.
7. Tape the packets to the record. Make sure the edge on each packet labeled "Center" is placed closest to the center of the record. Place the record on the turntable.
8. Turn the turntable on at the lowest speed. Leave it on for five days. Every other day, open the foil packets and make sure the paper towels haven't dried out. If they seem dry, carefully add a little water but do not disturb the seeds in any way.
9. After five days, open the packets. Record what direction the roots are growing in with respect to the edge of the packet that was facing the center of the turntable.

What you should notice:

◆ All the roots will grow away from the edge of the packet that was facing the center of the turntable.

Here's what's happening:

In "Finding Down" on page 97, you will prove that geotropism plays a big role in how plants grow. In this experiment, however, the roots don't grow down toward the center of the earth—they grow out away from the center of the turntable. The reason for this is a process called *gravitropism*.

Gravitropism is the growth of a plant in response to the direction of the strongest force acting on it. In most cases, gravitropism is the same as geotropism, because for most plants, the force of gravity is the strongest force they experience. In this experiment, however, the rotation of the turntable exerts a force on the growing seeds.

When the turntable spins, objects on the turntable experience a force called *centripetal force*. This force fools the growing seeds—instead of growing in response to the force of the earth's gravity, they grow in response to the centripetal force they feel. This makes the roots grow outward from the center of the turntable. If you repeated this experiment without turning the turntable on, you would see the roots grow in random directions, trying to find their way down.

Tinting Flowers
Give your flowers a makeover.

This is what you'll need:

Some red, pink, or purple flowers
Some white or yellow flowers
String
A drinking straw
Household ammonia
A jar with a lid
Tape
Scissors
Safety Warning: Be careful when handling chemicals
like ammonia, since direct contact can be harmful.

Here's what to do:

1. Tie the flowers together into a bunch with the string. Leave a few inches of string hanging off one end.
2. Tie the string to the drinking straw so the flowers hang down from the straw.
3. Pour a thin layer of ammonia into the bottom of the jar.
4. Hang the bunch of flowers into the jar by balancing the straw over the mouth of the jar. Tape the straw into place. Cut off the ends of the straw.
5. Replace the lid on the jar. Don't worry if you can't screw it into place. Tape the lid onto the jar to minimize any ammonia vapors escaping.
6. After an hour, examine the flowers, recording any color changes you see.

What you should notice:

◆ The red, pink, or purple flowers should lose their color and take on a faint green tint.
◆ The white or yellow flowers should be unaffected.

Here's what's happening:

The dyes that give a flower its colors are chemicals, and like any other chemicals, they can be affected by changes in pH. Different acids and bases can cause chemical changes in the dyes. Ammonia is a base, and when ammonia vapor comes in contact with red, pink, or purple plant dyes, they undergo a chemical change that makes the dyes transparent. Those flowers then appear green, not because the chemical change has produced a green dye, but because the cells in the flower petals contain chlorophyll that is now able to show through. The dyes in white and yellow flowers are usually unaffected by ammonia.

Dig a little deeper:

If you look carefully at different kinds of white flowers, you may notice that some have a greenish tint to them. This tint is often caused by the chlorophyll in the cells showing through.

Things to try:

→ Repeat this experiment using colored paper instead of flowers. How are the dyes used in papermaking affected by ammonia?

Bleached Leaves
Get rid of that green.

This is what you'll need:

Water
A saucepan
Leaves from different plants and trees
Tweezers or tongs
1 cup rubbing alcohol
Safety Warning: Be careful when handling alcohol, since direct
contact can be harmful. Have an adult supervise when
using the stove.

Here's what to do:

1. Pour the water into the saucepan and bring it to a gentle boil. You may want an adult's help for this.
2. Add the leaves, and boil them for 5 to 10 minutes.
3. Carefully remove the leaves from the water with tweezers or tongs (you can rest them on some paper towels). Pour the water down the sink.
4. Pour the alcohol into the saucepan and bring it to a gentle boil.
5. Boil the leaves in the alcohol for 10 to 15 minutes, until they become transparent.
6. Carefully remove the leaves from the alcohol with tweezers or tongs. Examine them closely.

What you should notice:

◆ Green color should seep into the alcohol while you boil the leaves.
◆ The leaves will be transparent when you remove them from the alcohol.

Here's what's happening:

The pigment that gives plant cells their green color, chlorophyll, is held inside structures known as *chloroplasts*. To remove the chlorophyll from a plant cell, you have to break the cell wall and the membranes of the chloroplasts. Boiling the leaves in water weakens the cell walls, and boiling them in alcohol breaks the chloroplast membranes. As you boil the leaves in alcohol, the liquid becomes more and more green in color—this is caused by the chlorophyll leaking out. The rest of the leaf is still intact, so when you remove a leaf from the boiling alcohol, it appears transparent but otherwise perfect.

Things to try:

→ Examine a bleached leaf under a microscope. Do you notice differences between bleached leaves and regular leaves?

Plant Grafting
Can you graft two different plants together?

This is what you'll need:

2 plants, about 10 inches tall, grown from kidney
     beans, each in its own pot
2 plants, about 10 inches tall, grown from lima beans,
     each in its own pot
A paring knife
Modeling clay
Kitchen twine
Red and blue food coloring
Water
Paper cups

*Note: You can use any kinds of bean plants you want for this experiment—
just make sure the plants are each at least 10 inches tall (taller is okay).
Using different plants makes a dramatic display at the science fair, since two
different types of leaves will be visible on one stem, but you can also use two
of the same type of plant to demonstrate the principles of this experiment.*
Safety Warning: Have an adult supervise when using the paring knife.

Here's what to do:

1. Pair one kidney bean plant with one lima bean plant and place the pots next to each other.

2. Figure out where the graft will be by pulling the two main stems together and finding a spot where they comfortably touch.

3. At this spot, shave the stem of each plant a little bit with the paring knife, just enough to expose the inside of the stem.

4. Hold the shaved stems together and wrap some modeling clay around them to hold them in place.

5. For extra stability, wrap some kitchen twine around the stems above and below the graft.

6. Repeat this process for the other pair of plants.

7. Dilute five drops of red food coloring in one cup of water, and five drops of blue food coloring in another cup of water. Over the course of the experiment, water the pots of kidney bean plants with red water and lima bean plants with blue water.

8. Observe the plants every day for signs of damage, like yellowing or withering. Record what kind of a difference the food coloring makes in the appearance of the plants.

9. After one week, check the plants to make sure they are healthy. If they are, on one pair, snip off the bottom of the kidney bean plant and the top of the lima bean plant. Do the opposite on the other pair.

10. Continue watering the plants with colored water as before. Observe the plants every day for two weeks. Does the grafted part survive? Does it grow at the same rate as the rest of the plant? Does it get an equal amount of water? It is the same color as the rest of the plant?

What you should notice:

◆ When the grafts are successful and both plants are attached, the kidney bean plants should take on a red tinge and the lima bean plants should take on a blue tinge, but the branches and leaves above the graft site should look more purple.

◆ When the grafts are successful, the grafted leaves and branches should thrive even after the bottom plant is cut off.

Here's what's happening:

When you get a cut, your body is able to heal itself over time. A similar process happens in plants—for example, when you cut a flower off a plant, the plant actually sustains an injury. The injury does not usually kill the plant, though, because it heals the injured area. In this experiment, you are taking advantage of a plant's ability to heal its damaged tissues.

By shaving the stems of the plants, you injured them enough to start the process of healing. When you placed the two open "wounds" together, the plants healed around each other. The xylem and phloem supply tubes that were cut on each plant became reconnected, but they reconnected to whatever tube was closest. Often, for example, the bottom half of the kidney bean plant's xylem connected up with the top half of the lima bean plant's xylem. In this way, the plants were able to share resources from each set of roots within the grafted branches and leaves. Since xylem runs from both sets of roots into the graft, the grafted area takes on color from the red and blue water. (For an explanation of how colored water moves through the xylem to tint a plant, see "Rainbow Flowers" on page 81.) Even after the bottom half of one plant is snipped off, the grafted leaves and branches are able to survive because they are able to get nutrients from the other plant's roots.

Things to try:

→ Experiment with different "wounds." Shave some stems deeper, or make the cuts longer, or make cuts in different places (like the main stem of one plant and a leaf stem of another). What are the best conditions for grafting?

A-"Maze"ing Beans

Can a plant find its way through a maze?

This is what you'll need:

Scissors
A shoe box
Cardboard
Tape
2 or 3 sprouting bean plants
Soil
A paper cup

Here's what to do:

1. Cut two small holes on opposite walls of the shoe box.
2. Cut squares and rectangles from the cardboard and tape them to the inside of the box to make a maze. Build some "dead ends" into the maze. (See the illustration below.)

Open to the sun

3. Plant the bean sprouts in some soil in the paper cup and position the plants so they fit through one of the holes in the shoebox.
4. Replace the shoe box lid and place the box somewhere that some sunlight can get through the opposite hole.
5. Every other day, open the lid and see how the plants are growing. Are they able to find the end of the maze?

What you should notice:

◆ The plants will grow through the maze toward the light source, avoiding the dead ends.

Here's what's happening:

This experiment demonstrates a process known as *phototropism*. The shoots of most plants will grow toward a light source, even when it is hard to reach. The bean plants in this experiment will twist and turn through the maze to get as close to the light source as possible. In fact, you may have noticed that over time, the plants avoid all the dead ends in the maze. Since there is no light in the dead ends, the plants avoid them to reach the light source.

Phototropism can be positive (growth proceeds toward the light source) or negative (growth moves away from the light source). As you've seen in this experiment, the shoots of the plants are *positively phototropic*. The roots, however, are a different story. Most roots grow away from light and dig themselves deeper into the earth over time. Roots are *negatively phototropic*.

Dig a little deeper:

Originally, phototropism was called heliotropism—growth of a plant toward the sun. This term was altered when it became clear that plants would grow toward artificial sources of light.

Things to try:

→ Change the light source over the course of the experiment by sealing one hole and cutting a new one in the box. What happens to the growing plant?

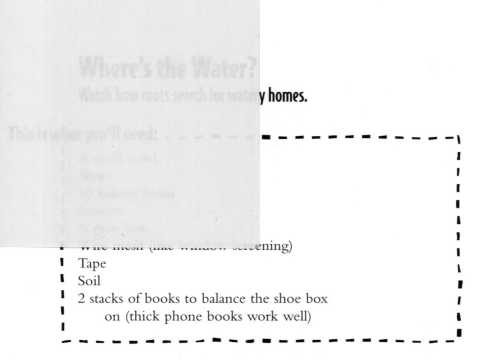

Where's the Water?
Watch how roots search for watery homes.

This is what you'll need:

- A small bowl
- Water
- 10 kidney beans
- Scissors
- A shoe box
- Wire mesh (like window screening)
- Tape
- Soil
- 2 stacks of books to balance the shoe box on (thick phone books work well)

Here's what to do:

1. Fill the bowl with water and submerge the kidney beans.
2. Let the beans soak in the water overnight in the refrigerator.
3. The next day, cut two small holes (1 inch in diameter) in the bottom of the shoe box at opposite ends.
4. Cut pieces of wire mesh to cover the holes and tape the mesh into place.
5. Fill the box with soil so it is at least 3 inches deep.
6. Plant the soaked kidney beans in the soil, making sure they are covered.
7. Water the soil a little bit so it is moist. Do not overwater the plants in this experiment!
8. Stack the books up and balance the shoe box across the stacks. (See the illustration of the setup on the following page, so you can see how it's put together.) Make sure the stacks are high enough for you to place a small bowl under one of the holes in the shoe box (the box should sit about ½ inch above the top of the bowl).
9. Fill the bowl with water and place it under one of the holes in the shoe box. Make sure there is nothing under the other hole.
10. Let the beans grow for two weeks. Every day, observe what happens to the roots.

What you should notice:

◆ Over time, the roots extend out through the hole above the bowl of water.
◆ Any roots that extend out through the hole that has no water under it soon turn around and point back into the soil.

Here's what's happening:

This experiment demonstrates a process known as *hydrotropism*. The roots of most plants will grow toward a source of water, even when it is hard to reach. Most of the roots of the plants in this experiment will grow toward the hole above the bowl of water. Even the roots of the beans that were planted far away would eventually find their way to the water source.

Those roots that had extended out through the hole that had no water under it eventually turned around and buried themselves in the soil. This is because the soil had more moisture than the air; the roots preferred being in the soil to open air.

Finding Down
Do plants know which way is down?

This is what you'll need:

6 small glass panes from photo frames
Paper towels
9 sprouting bean plants, about 2 inches long
Modeling clay
Rubber bands
Water

Here's what to do:

1. Place three of the glass panes on a flat surface. Fold some paper towels and place them on the glass panes.

2. Place three sprouting bean plants on each paper towel, making sure the plants are aligned with roots pointing in the same direction.

3. Position a small gob of modeling clay over each stem (this will help keep the plants in place).

4. Position two long strips of modeling clay on the glass panes, one on each side of the paper towels. Make sure the strips are at least as thick as the plants. (See the illustration above.)

5. Place another glass pane over the plants. Secure the panes together with rubber bands.

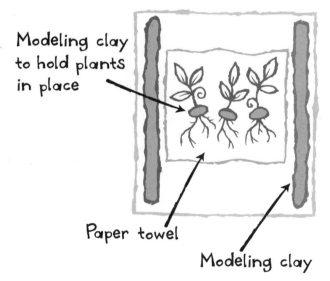

Modeling clay to hold plants in place

Paper towel

Modeling clay

6. Prop the setups upright in a dark area so that one set of plants has its roots pointing down, one set has its roots pointing up, and one set has its roots pointing horizontally. (See the illustration below.)

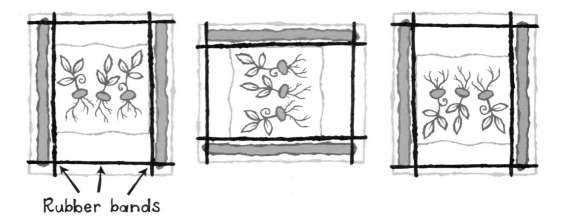

Rubber bands

7. Water the plants whenever the paper towels start to dry out.
8. Observe what happens to the roots of the plants in the different setups for at least one week.

What you should notice:

◆ Over time, the roots turn to point downward.

Here's what's happening:

This experiment demonstrates a process known as *geotropism*. The roots of most plants will grow toward the center of the earth—no matter what their previous direction of growth was. Even the plants placed in a maze upside down will eventually reverse so their roots point downward.

Geotropism, just like phototropism, can be positive or negative. Roots are *positively geotropic*, and shoots, which grow upward, are *negatively geotropic*.

HEAT IT UP

Some Like It Hot
Can a simple chemical reaction raise the temperature by a few degrees?

This is what you'll need:

¼ cup hydrogen peroxide (available at
    drugstores)
A paper cup
A scientific thermometer (available at
    science supply stores)
1 tablespoon quick-rising dry yeast (available
    at grocery stores)

*Safety Warning: Be careful when handling chemicals
like hydrogen peroxide, since direct contact can be harmful.*

Here's what to do:

1. Pour the hydrogen peroxide into the paper cup.
2. Use the thermometer to determine the temperature of the hydrogen peroxide.
3. Record the temperature in the chart on the next page.
4. Add the quick-rising dry yeast to the hydrogen peroxide and stir.
5. Feel the sides of the cups with your hands. Record any temperature changes you notice.
6. After one or two minutes, take the temperature of the hydrogen peroxide–yeast mixture. Record the temperature in the chart.

What you should notice:

◆ When the hydrogen peroxide mixes with the yeast, the temperature of the mixture increases.

Here's what's happening:

This experiment is an example of an *exothermic reaction*. The word *exothermic* means that heat is released when the reaction takes place. The mixture of hydrogen peroxide and yeast yields oxygen gas (which can be seen as bubbles escaping from the solution), water, and heat.

In this chemical reaction, the yeast only acts as a *catalyst*—it helps to speed the reaction along, but doesn't actually undergo any chemical change. The hydrogen peroxide, on the other hand, undergoes a *decomposition reaction*. The chemical equation for hydrogen peroxide is H_2O_2, meaning each molecule of hydrogen peroxide is made up of two atoms of hydrogen and two atoms of oxygen. When hydrogen peroxide decomposes, it breaks down into water (H_2O) and oxygen gas (O_2). During the breakdown, heat is released, and you can feel the temperature increase of the solution with your hands or measure it with the thermometer.

Things to try:

→ Use double the amount of hydrogen peroxide and yeast. Does the temperature rise more than when less hydrogen peroxide and yeast were used?

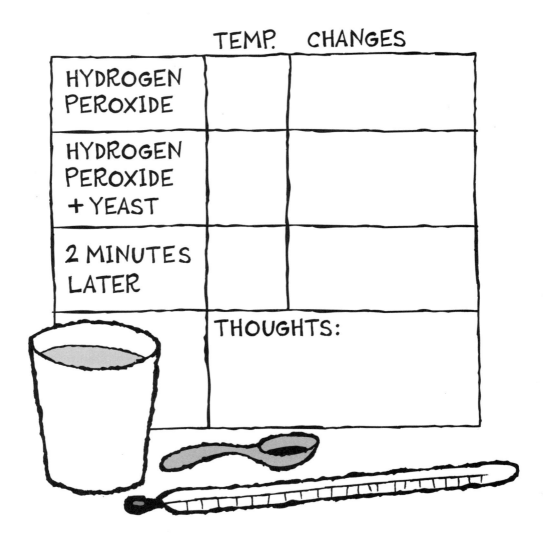

And Some Like It Cold

Can chemistry cool things down too?

This is what you'll need:

A paper cup
Room-temperature water
A scientific thermometer (available at
        science supply stores)
1 tablespoon Epsom salts, (available at
        drugstores)
Safety Warning: Be careful when handling chemicals
like Epsom salts, since direct contact can be harmful.

Here's what to do:

1. Pour tepid water into the paper cup, filling it about halfway.
2. Use the thermometer to determine the temperature of the water. Record the temperature.
3. Add the Epsom salts to the cup of water and stir.
4. Feel the side of the cup with your hands. Record any temperature changes you notice.
5. After one or two minutes, take the temperature of the Epsom salt–water mixture. Record the temperature.

What you should notice:

◆ When the Epsom salts mix with the water, the temperature of the mixture decreases.

Here's what's happening:

This experiment can be thought of as the opposite of the previous chemical reaction. Instead of heat being released when the chemical reaction takes place, heat is used to cause the reaction to occur. This is an example of an *endothermic reaction*. *Endothermic* means heat is absorbed. Epsom salts are really magnesium sulfate, a type of salt. When mixed with water, the magnesium sulfate uses heat to split into ions of magnesium and sulfate in order to dissolve into the water. Since the reaction uses heat, the temperature of the water drops.

Dig a little deeper:

Whenever chemical bonds are made or broken, energy is involved—either energy is used or it is released. With magnesium sulfate, energy is used up (and therefore heat is absorbed) when the chemical bonds between the magnesium ions and sulfate ions are broken. With a different salt like calcium chloride, energy is released when the chemical bonds between ions are broken (and therefore heat is released).

Things to try:

→ Use double the amount of Epsom salts. Does the temperature decrease more than when less Epsom salts were used?

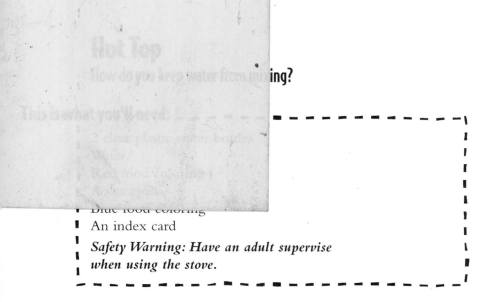

ing?

▪ Blue food coloring
▪ An index card
▪ *Safety Warning: Have an adult supervise when using the stove.*

Here's what to do:

1. Fill one bottle with water and add some red food coloring. Place this bottle in the refrigerator for one hour.
2. When the hour is almost up, heat enough water in a saucepan to fill the other bottle. Don't let the water boil, but make sure it gets pretty hot.
3. With an adult's help, fill the other bottle with the water you heated. Add some blue food coloring.
4. Take the red water bottle out of the fridge. Place it on a flat work surface.
5. Hold the index card over the top of the blue bottle. Quickly invert it over the red bottle and line up the bottle openings.
6. When the openings are perfectly aligned, carefully slide the index card out from between the bottles.
7. In the chart on the next page, record what happens to the two colors of water.

What you should notice:

◆ The cold, red water stays on the bottom and the hot, blue water stays on the top.

Here's what's happening:

This experiment takes advantage of the effect of temperature on density. A colder liquid is more dense than a warmer liquid. The molecules in cold water move around less than the molecules in hot water. They have less energy to use for motion because the temperature is lower. Because the cold water molecules move less, more molecules can be packed into the same total volume than in the case of hot water. This makes cold water more dense than hot water.

Because of the difference in density, the hot water tends to float on top of the cold water rather than mix with it. This is why the colors seem to stay separate. The longer the hot and cold water are left in contact, the closer in temperature they become. Then the red and blue water will begin to mix.

Things to try:

→ Demonstrate the difference between the amount of motion in the molecules of hot water versus cold water by adding three drops of food coloring to a cup of refrigerated water and three drops of food coloring to a cup of heated water. In which cup does the color blend first?

COLOR	CHANGES
RED BOTTLE	
BLUE BOTTLE	

Colder than Freezing
How can water be colder than 32°F and still not be frozen?

This is what you'll need:

2 ziplock bags
Water
Crushed ice (enough to fill 2 coffee cans), or
    ice cubes and an adult to crush them for you
2 empty coffee cans with lids
6 tablespoons rock salt
A marker
A thermometer (available at science
    supply stores)

Here's what to do:

1. Fill the ziplock bags with water and seal them.
2. Fill the coffee cans halfway with ice and then place one sealed ziplock bag of water in each.
3. Cover one bag in crushed ice until the coffee can is completely full and put on the lid.
4. Add the rock salt to the other coffee can, label it "Salt Added," and fill it the rest of the way with crushed ice. Put on the lid.
5. Roll both cans back and forth for 15 minutes.
6. Use the thermometer to take the temperature of the mixture in each coffee can. Record these temperatures.
7. Take the ziplock bags out and examine the water inside. Record whether the water is frozen, and any differences in the amount of freezing between the two samples. Open the bags and take the temperature of the water inside. Record these temperatures.

What you should notice:

◆ The ice water–salt mixture inside the "Salt Added" can water is colder than the ice-water mixture in the other can.
◆ After 15 minutes, the water inside the ziplock bag in the "Salt Added" can has frozen where the water inside the other bag has not.

Here's what's happening:

Water with ice in it—any amount of ice—will stay at a constant temperature of 32°F. Although this is the freezing point of water, unless the temperature is lowered below the freezing point, the water won't change to a solid state—it will remain a liquid. The moment the temperature falls below 32°F, though, the water will change states and solidify.

When salt is added to water, it changes the freezing point of the liquid, lowering it by several degrees. By adding salt to the coffee can of ice and water, the ice water–salt mixture was able to stay at a constant temperature that was below the freezing point of water. Although the ice water–salt mixture stayed liquid, the pure water inside the ziplock bag was able to freeze because the temperature fell below 32°F.

Dig a little deeper:

The phenomenon demonstrated here is called *freezing point depression*. One real application of this happens every winter. When it snows, salt trucks are sent out to lay salt onto major roads. The salt mixes with the melting snow and lowers the freezing point. This way, the roads do not become icy when the temperature drops.

Things to try:

→ Try using sugar instead of salt. How does this affect the freezing point of water?

Spinning Snake

Make this paper snake spin using just a lightbulb.

This is what you'll need:

A pencil
Paper
Scissors
Thread
A sewing needle
A desk lamp with an adjustable neck (make sure
    you can adjust it so that the light points up)

Here's what to do:

1. Draw a spiral snake on the piece of paper and cut it out. Make sure the snake is at least 5 inches in diameter.

2. Cut a length of thread about 12 inches long. Thread the needle and pull the needle and thread through the snake's "eye." Knot the thread so you can use it to hold the snake up.
3. Adjust the desk lamp so that the light points up.
4. Hold the piece of thread so that the snake hangs about 3 or 4 inches above the lightbulb. Do not let the snake touch the bulb directly.
5. Hold your hands as still as possible and watch what happens to the snake.

What you should notice:

◆ After a few moments, the spiral snake begins to spin.

Here's what's happening:

The lightbulb produces both light and heat. The heat it produces warms the air around it. Since hot air is lighter than room-temperature air, the air around the lightbulb rises away from the lamp. Cooler air from the surroundings has to come in to replace the hot air that is rising away. Between the hot air rising and the cooler air rushing downward, a convection current is created. This causes the snake to spin.

Water Convection

Just as in air, temperature differences in water can cause
convection currents with colorful effects.

This is what you'll need:

- A paper cup
- Duct tape
- An aquarium water heater
- A small aquarium
- Water
- An eyedropper
- Blue food coloring
- Ice cubes, tinted red with food coloring
    before freezing

Here's what to do:

1. Poke a few small holes in the paper cup. Tape it to the inside of the aquarium using duct tape.
2. Place the aquarium water heater on the opposite side of the aquarium. Try to make sure that both the paper cup and the water heater are at the same level and are placed roughly midway up the aquarium side.
3. Fill the aquarium with enough water to cover the holes in the bottom of the paper cup and at least part of the water heater. Do not submerge the paper cup or else the ice cubes will float out!
4. Fill the eyedropper with blue food coloring.
5. Place the red ice cubes in the paper cup.
6. Turn the heater on.
7. Use the dropper to place a few drops of blue food coloring in the water near the heater. Make sure the tip of the dropper is submerged when you release the blue food coloring. (See illustration on following page to see how the setup looks.)
8. Observe how the red and blue colors flow and record your observations.

What you should notice:

◆ The red color should drift downward and toward the heater.
◆ The blue color should drift upward and toward the paper cup.

Here's what's happening:

Just as hot air rises, hot water rises as well. The drops of blue food coloring get heated by the aquarium heater, and the heat makes the blue water less dense than the rest of the water in the aquarium, so the blue water rises at first. But as the blue water gets closer to the ice cubes, it begins to cool down. This increases the density of the blue water, and it starts to sink.

The red ice cubes melt inside the aquarium, and the red-colored water is colder and denser than the rest of the water in the aquarium. At first, the red water sinks to the bottom of the aquarium. As the red water gets closer to the heater, it begins to heat up. This decreases the density of the red water, and it starts to rise.

Together, the motion of the warmer water in one direction and the cooler water in the opposite direction creates a convection current, just as we saw in the air in "Spinning Snake" on page 107. Since the colored water will dilute inside the tank, you won't be able to see the colors cycling continuously. But the convection current continues even after the color has disappeared. You can add more red ice cubes and blue drops to watch the current cycle again.

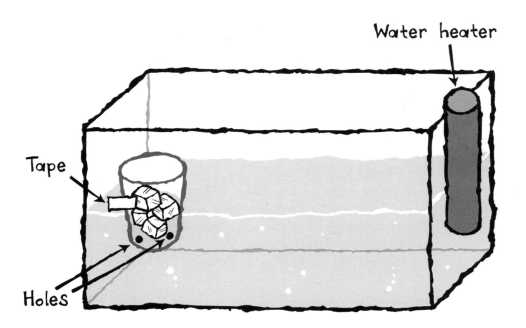

Hot Wood, Cold Metal
Are your hands good thermometers?

This is what you'll need:

A block of wood
A metal cookie sheet
A large piece of cardboard

A large piece of Styrofoam
Liquid crystal thermometer cards

Here's what to do:

1. Arrange the wood, cookie sheet, cardboard, and Styrofoam on a tabletop.
2. Place the palm of one hand on one object and the other on another. Try to arrange the objects in order from the one that feels the coldest to the one that feels the warmest.
3. Use the liquid crystal thermometer cards to check the temperature of the different objects. Lay a thermometer card flat on each object and wait 15 seconds for the temperature to register (the color will change).

What you should notice:

◆ No matter what your hands tell you, all the objects are at the same temperature according to the thermometers.

Here's what's happening:

The nerves in your skin are designed to detect temperature by determining whether your body heat is being taken away or whether your body heat is being held in place when you touch something. When you touch a good heat conductor, like a piece of metal, your body heat is easily conducted away. These materials feel colder to your hands than good heat insulators. Examples of heat insulators are wood and Styrofoam. When you touch one of these materials, your body heat is held in place because the insulators prevent the heat from escaping. These materials feel warmer to your hands. Even though in reality, all these materials are at room temperature, some feel warmer or colder based on their ability to conduct or insulate heat. Differences in the rate at which a conductor carries heat away or at which an insulator keeps heat explains why even different conductors or insulators may feel as if they are different temperatures.

Things to try:

→ Try different thicknesses of the same material, like different thicknesses of Styrofoam or metal. Can you detect a difference in conducting or insulating ability based on thickness?

Cut a Cube

Cut an ice cube in half without lifting a finger.

This is what you'll need:

Copper wire
Scissors or wire cutters
10 thick metal washers
An ice cube
A tall can or wood block
Modeling clay

Here's what to do:

1. Cut a piece of copper wire about the height of the can.
2. Tie the metal washers on each end of the wire, 5 on each side.
3. Place the ice cube on top of the can and put some modeling clay around it to keep it from sliding off the top.
4. Position the wire across the center of the ice cube so the metal washers are hanging off the edge of the can. (See the illustration below.)
5. Sit back and relax—and wait for the wire to cut through the ice cube. It may take 10 or 15 minutes, but it will work.

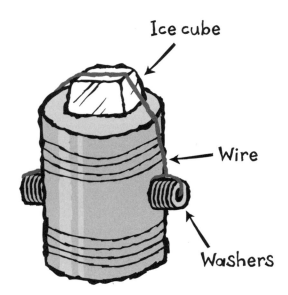

Ice cube

Wire

Washers

What you should notice:

◆ After a while, the wire "cuts" through the ice cube.

Here's what's happening:

The washers in this experiment weigh the wire down, so the wire is pressing on the surface of the ice cube. The parts of the ice cube directly pressed on by the wire melt at a faster rate than the rest of the ice cube. This is because melting temperatures are dependent on pressure.

Normally, the melting point of ice is determined by atmospheric pressure, which is the pressure that the air around us exerts on everything. When ice is placed under increased pressure—as is the case when the weighted-down wire presses on the ice cube—it can melt at a lower temperature than it would at atmospheric pressure. In this way, the wire is able to cut through the ice cube easily.

This experiment works with ice because of a unique property of water. For most things, the melting point actually increases with pressure. The more pressure you put on it, the higher the temperature required to melt it. However, the density of ice is less than that of liquid water. This is why the melting point of ice decreases with pressure.

Dig a little deeper:

The same principles demonstrated here apply to ice-skating. When a person skates on ice, the person's weight is distributed on the blade, which exerts pressure on the ice. The ice directly below the blade tends to melt more quickly than the rest of the ice rink surface. This is what allows the ice-skater to move across the ice.

Things to try:

→ Try this experiment again, but instead of wire use string, which does not conduct heat well. Do you get two solid blocks after the string cuts through the ice cube? Why doesn't the ice cube refreeze when you use string instead of wire?

Solar Oven

Can you make s'mores in a pizza box? Using simple things from around the house, you can transform a pizza box into a solar oven.

This is what you'll need:

- A marker
- A ruler
- A pizza box
- Scissors
- Aluminum foil
- Glue
- Clear, heavy plastic sheets (like the kind used to cover books)
- Black construction paper
- An oven thermometer
- A drinking straw

Here's what to do:

1. Draw a square with a 2-inch border on the top of the pizza box.
2. Cut along three sides of the border so that there is a flap in the top of the box.

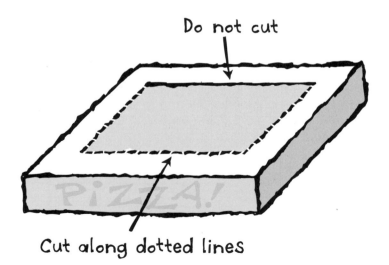

Do not cut

Cut along dotted lines

3. Cut out two pieces of aluminum foil to line the bottom of the pizza box and to cover the inside face of the flap. Glue one piece on the bottom of the pizza box directly under the window created by opening the flap, and the other to the underside of the flap (the pieces of foil will face each other when the flap is closed).

4. Cut out a piece of clear plastic larger than the window you cut out in the top of the pizza box. Glue it to the top of the pizza box so that you can still open and close the flap above the plastic. (If you can't find heavy clear plastic sheets, you can used kitchen cling wrap—just be careful not to puncture it, as it is considerably more fragile.)

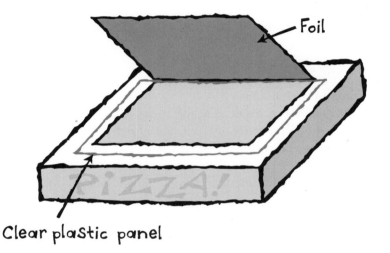

Foil

Clear plastic panel

5. Layer some black construction paper over the foil in the bottom of the box and glue it in place.

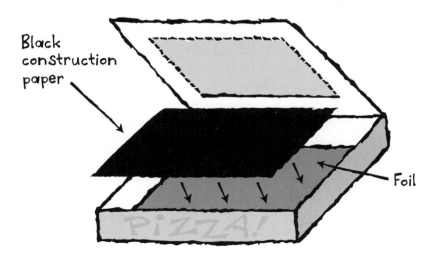

Black construction paper

Foil

6. Place the oven thermometer inside the pizza box and close the top. You should be able to see the thermometer through the plastic window.
7. Place the pizza box facing the sun. Prop the flap open, using the straw if necessary. Adjust the flap so that the maximum amount of sunlight is reflected into the box through the plastic window.

What you should notice:

◆ What is the maximum temperature your solar oven reaches? Don't be surprised if this simple solar oven reaches 200°F.

Here's what's happening:

The pizza box oven you built is able to get hot for two reasons. First, there is insulation in the oven that keeps the heat inside it. The pizza box and the plastic panel trap air inside the oven. The air gets heated by the sunlight, but cannot escape. Some energy transfer can take place at the edges of the box (where the hot air cools down because it is close to the cooler air outside), but the cardboard walls of the pizza box insulate against energy loss.

Second, the solar oven you built demonstrates the principle of *solar gain*. This means you've arranged for the energy source of the oven to be sunlight, and you gain the energy directly (by letting sunlight into the box through the plastic window) and through reflection (from sunlight being bounced off the foil panel into the oven). Also, the dark construction paper increases the solar gain by absorbing the solar energy that enters the oven.

As a result, the solar oven is able to get pretty hot using fairly simple materials.

Dig a little deeper:

Solar ovens have been used for thousands of years. If you remove the reflector flap, the rest of the solar oven is referred to as a flat plate collector. One of the first instances of solar ovens being used was in the household of the Roman emperor Tiberius. Tiberius wanted to eat cucumbers all year round, but cucumbers would not normally grow in the winter. His cooks, however, devised a way to use flat plate collectors to grow cucumbers even when it got very cold outside.

Things to try:

→ Add crumpled-up newspapers to the inside of the solar oven to add more insulation. What is the maximum temperature the solar oven can now reach?

FALLING AND FLOATING

Which Fell First, the Chicken or the Egg?
Answer another age-old question about gravity.

This is what you'll need:

- A piece of cooked chicken, like a chicken nugget or chicken wing
- A kitchen scale
- A hard-boiled egg, peeled
- A feather

Here's what to do:

1. Weigh the piece of chicken and the egg and record their weights.
2. Stand outside on the grass or inside on an easy-to-clean floor. Hold the piece of chicken in one hand and the egg in the other. Hold your hands out at your sides at the same height.
3. Let go of both objects at the same time. Record which one hits the ground first.
4. Repeat the experiment, this time replacing the egg with the feather. Let go of both items at the same time. Record which one hits the ground first.
5. Now hold the feather and the piece of chicken in the same hand, but hold the feather right on top of the chicken. Let go of both of them and record how the feather falls this time.

What you should notice:

- The piece of chicken and the egg hit the ground at the some time.
- When the chicken and feather are held far apart and then dropped, the piece of chicken hits the ground first.
- When the feather is held directly above the piece of chicken, both items hit the ground at the same time.

Here's what's happening:

On earth, everything falls down. The force of gravity acts on objects, pulling them toward the center of the earth. Believe it or not, the size or weight of an object has no effect on the rate that the object accelerates as it falls.

Galileo predicted that objects of different weights would fall to the ground at the same time. He reasoned that a falling object was pulled by gravity—the heavier an object is, the harder the earth pulls on it. But he also reasoned that it is easier to accelerate a lighter object than a heavier one. Therefore, if object A is 10 times heavier than object B, the gravitational pull on A will be 10 times greater, but 10 times harder to accelerate. These effects essentially cancel out, and all objects fall down at the same rate.

Of course, this doesn't mean that all objects dropped from the same height always hit the ground at the same time. Galileo's predictions, and the law of gravity, hold true in a vacuum—a situation where no other forces act on the falling objects. In the real world, all sorts of forces can act on a falling object. For example, air resistance is the reason that the feather falls more slowly than the chicken or the egg. Air resistance is a type of friction that interferes with an object's downward motion.

All objects experience air resistance, but its effect is more dramatic on some, like the feather, than others, like the chicken. This has to do with how the air resistance experienced by an object compares with the gravitational pull acting on it. In the cases of the chicken and the egg, the air resistance is small compared to the gravitational force, and thus does not play a large role in the rate those things fall. In the case of the feather, the air resistance is significant and dramatically slows the feather's falling speed.

When you hold the feather on top of the chicken and drop them both together, the chicken "shields" the feather from air resistance. In this case, you can assume that both objects are experiencing the same amount of air resistance, and therefore hit the ground at the same time.

Dig a little deeper:

Even though objects fall at the same rate, the rate is not constant throughout the fall. The reason for this is the relationship between speed and acceleration.

The gravitational pull of the earth accelerates falling objects at the rate of 9.8 m/sec^2. The longer something falls, the more it accelerates. The speed at which an object falls is dependent on the rate at which it is accelerated and the time it takes in transit. (It also depends on the speed it is moving initially, but in this experiment, since the objects are being dropped from rest, the initial speed is zero.) Mathematically, the equation is:

$$\text{Speed = Acceleration} \times \text{Time}$$

In the case of a falling object, the speed it is falling after one second would be 9.8 m/sec^2 x 1 sec = 9.8 m/sec. After two seconds, its speed is 19.6 m/sec.

In this experiment, you may be able to notice that the falling chicken gains speed as it falls.

Racing Jars
Will the heavy jar or the light jar reach the bottom of the ramp first?

This is what you'll need:

2 cylindrical jars with lids
Water
A plank of wood to make a ramp
Phone books (or anything that can be used to
    prop one end of the ramp up)

Here's what to do:

1. Fill one jar with water. Screw the lids tight on both jars.
2. Make a ramp with the stack of phone books and the plank of wood (you could also prop one side of the plank up on a staircase step).
3. Hold both jars at the top of the ramp. Predict which one will roll faster.
4. Release the jars. Record which jar reaches the bottom of the ramp first.

What you should notice:

◆ At first, the jar full of water rolls faster.
◆ As the race continues, the water jar slows down and the other jar wins the race.

Here's what's happening:

Before you started the race, you may have assumed that the jar filled with water would have won because it was heavier. And actually, when the two jars first start rolling, the water jar does roll faster. However, it rolls faster not because it is heavier, but because its weight is evenly distributed. The "empty" jar (which is actually not empty but full of air) is heaviest at its edges and therefore has a nonuniform weight distribution. It is initially harder to accelerate the empty jar than the full jar.

As the race continues, however, the jar filled with water slows down. Because it is heavier than the empty jar, the water jar experiences more friction between it and the ramp, which hinders its speed. The more mass an object has, the more friction it experiences. Since the empty jar is less hindered by friction, as the race continues, it rolls faster. The empty jar wins the race at the end.

Things to try:

→ Try reducing the friction between the jars and the ramp by using a slick material for the ramp or by adding a lubricant like oil to the ramp. Does the empty jar still win the race?
→ Experiment with raising and lowering the ramp. Do different inclinations change the outcome of the race?

Which Tin Will Win?

The distribution of weight in an object affects how fast it rolls down a ramp.

This is what you'll need:

Tape
10 heavy metal washers (you may need
    a few more or a few less)
2 round metal cookie tins with replaceable
    lids (shallow tins work best)
Phone books (or anything that can be
    used to prop one end of the ramp up)
A plank of wood to make a ramp

Here's what to do:

1. Tape five metal washers together into one long stack. Keep the other five loose.
2. Take the lids off the cookie tins. Tape the stack of washers inside one cookie tin, making sure the stack is centered. Replace the lid. (**Note:** If the lid won't fit with a stack of five washers, remove enough washers to be able to replace the lid. If there is a large gap between the top of the stack and the top of the cookie tin, add more washers to the stack.)
3. Take the same number of washers you used in the first cookie tin and tape them around the outer inside edge of the second cookie tin. Replace the lid. Make sure you use an equal numbers of washers in both cookie tins so that both weigh the same.
4. Make a ramp with the stack of books and the plank of wood.
5. Hold both cookie tins at the top of the ramp. Predict which one will roll faster.
6. Release the cookie tins. Record which one reaches the bottom of the ramp first.

What you should notice:

◆ The cookie tin that has the stack of washers in the center reaches the bottom of the ramp first.

Here's what's happening:

In "Racing Jars," on page 119, you discovered that a heavier object will roll more slowly down an incline because it experiences more friction. In this experiment, both cookie tins weigh the same, since they are each weighted by an equal number of washers, but the cookie tin with all the washers concentrated in the center always wins the cookie-tin race. The reason for this is that the energy it takes to rotate an object depends on its weight distribution.

Washers stacked

Washers evenly distributed

INSIDE VIEW of COOKIE TINS

At the top of the ramp, the cookie tins have the same amount of *potential energy*, meaning that they aren't moving, but they have a certain *potential* to move. When they begin rolling down the ramp, the potential energy gets transformed into *kinetic energy* (the energy of motion). Since one of the laws of physics is that energy is conserved, the total potential energy of each cookie tin equals its total kinetic energy. Since both tins start with the same amount of potential energy, the total kinetic energy they have is equal as well.

The total kinetic energy of the cookie tins when they are rolling comes in two parts: *translational* kinetic energy (the energy it takes to change positions; in this case, move from the top of the ramp to the bottom) and *rotational* kinetic energy (the energy it takes to rotate the tins as they roll). It takes more rotational kinetic energy to roll the cookie tin with the metal washers distributed around the edges—which means there is less energy available for moving. It takes less rotational kinetic energy to roll the other cookie tin with the washers concentrated in the center, leaving more energy available for moving. This cookie tin moves down the ramp faster and wins the race every time.

Dig a little deeper:

When an object rotates around an axis (as the cookie tins do when rolling down the ramp), how fast it rotates is determined by its *moment of inertia*. The moment of inertia is determined by the distribution of weight in the object. In this experiment, the cookie tin with the metal washers distributed around the edges has a higher moment of inertia that the other tin with the washers concentrated in the center. The higher moment of inertia explains why more rotational kinetic energy is required to roll this cookie tin.

Things to try:

→ Try using more washers in each cookie tin. Does the effect become more pronounced when the cookie tins weigh more?

Soap-Powered Boat: Give It Gas

Can you believe you can make a foil boat shoot across a surface of water like a rocket using only a bit of soap? Here's how.

This is what you'll need:

- A piece of aluminum foil with which to make your boat
- Scissors
- A large, flat dish (like a lasagna pan)
- Water
- A toothpick
- Dishwashing soap

Here's what to do:

1. Use the template given below to cut a "boat" out of a piece of foil. Carefully cut out the "well" in the back of the boat—this is where you are going to add the "fuel." Try to flatten the foil as much as possible with your fingernail. This will help your boat to float.

Template for the foil boat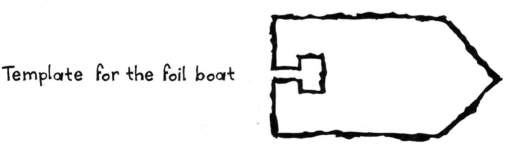

2. Fill the dish with water.
3. Float the boat on the water.
4. Dip a toothpick in some dishwashing soap. Gently touch the soapy end of the toothpick to the water inside the well. Try not to disturb the boat or the water.
5. Watch the boat shoot forward.

What you should notice:

◆ Look closely when you touch the soapy toothpick to the water—can you see the soap film spreading?

Here's what's happening:

Think about a balloon: if you fill it with air and then let it go, the air from inside the balloon shoots out the opening on one end and the balloon moves in the other direction. Something similar happens here, except with soap on water instead of air in air. When the soap comes in contact with the water, a thin film of soap is created. The soap molecules are trying to spread over the surface of the water. When the film has formed a layer that is one soap molecule thick (a monolayer), the boat stops moving.

Dig a little deeper:

Your boat is taking advantage of surface tension to "power" its motion. Water is a *polar molecule*. That means the hydrogen atoms and oxygen atom of a water molecule are arranged so that one side of the molecule is more negatively charged (the oxygen side) and the other side is more positively charged (the hydrogen side), like this one to the right.

When many water molecules come together, they tend to "stick" together. This happens because the hydrogen atoms in one molecule of water form connections, called *hydrogen bonds*, with the oxygen atoms of other water molecules. This forms sort of a net, like the one below.

The dotted lines in the drawing represent the hydrogen bonds. When the soap is placed in the well, it can only spread in one direction. As the soap molecules spread out the back of the well, the hydrogen bonds there get broken up. This makes the

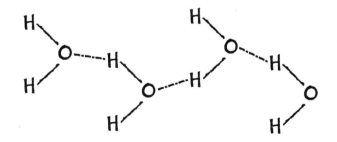

surface tension at the back of the boat different from that at the front of the boat. The result is that the boat is pushed forward.

Things to try:

➔ Use different types of soap to power the boat. Do liquid soaps work better than powdered soaps? What happens if you use oil instead of soap?

What Difference Does a Hull Make?

In the last experiment, you fueled a boat with soap. Now determine how the boat's shape affects its speed.

This is what you'll need:

- Aluminum foil to make your boats
- Scissors
- A large, flat dish like a lasagna pan
- A toothpick
- Dishwashing soap

Here's what to do:

1. Use the scissors and the foil to cut out a number of boats in different shapes. You can draw shapes of your own, or use the templates below. Remember to cut out a well for the soap "fuel" in the back of each boat.

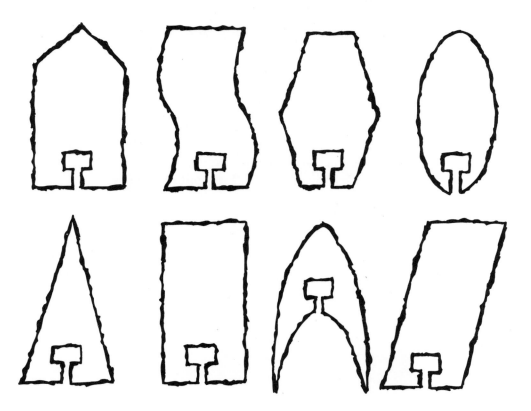

2. Fill the dish with water.
3. Place each boat in the water individually. Dip the toothpick in some dishwashing soap. Gently touch the soapy end of the toothpick to the water inside the well. Try not to disturb the boat or the water.
4. Watch the boat move and record how the water ripples. Note any differences in the ripple patterns among the different boats.
5. Place two boats in the water together. Dip soapy toothpicks into the water inside each well. Record which boat moves faster.

What you should notice:

◆ Do all the boats move forward?
◆ Were you able to notice any elements (pointy front, curved front, etc.) that made it easier for a boat to move faster?

Here's what's happening:

When something like a boat moves through water, the pattern of water flow at the front and the back of the boat plays a role in how well the boat moves. The more rippling you see in the water, the more resistance the boat is encountering, which will slow down the boat's progress. The water flow pattern around the front of the boat is called *drag*, and the pattern at the back is called *wake*. From your experiments, you should have noticed that boats with flat backs show the least amount of wake, and boats with wedge-shaped fronts show the least amount of drag.

Dig a little deeper:

The same principles used to design efficient hulls are used for other applications, like designing effective support pilings for bridges over bodies of water. Engineers carefully determine what shape will be most effective in reducing wear and tear due to water currents moving constantly against the pilings.

Things to try:

→ Pick the best boat shape. Repeat this experiment using this basic shape but altering each ship in one dimension (for example, make one boat the same width but longer, or make another the same length but wider). Compare the speeds of these boats against each other.

Cork at the Center

Can you guess where the cork will float?

This is what you'll need:

2 drinking glasses
Water
2 corks (if you can't find corks,
Styrofoam peanuts will work)

Here's what to do:

1. Fill the first drinking glass with water almost all the way to the rim.
2. Fill the other glass, and keep adding water until the water level is slightly above the rim of the glass.
3. Float one cork in the first glass. Record where it ends up.
4. Float the other cork in the second glass. Record where it ends up.

What you should notice:

◆ The cork floating in the glass where the water almost reaches the rim will always end up at an edge of the glass.

◆ The cork floating in the glass where the water level is slightly above the rim will always end up in the middle of the glass.

Here's what's happening:

The cork is less dense than the water, which is why the cork floats. It will always float where the water level is at its highest point.

In the first glass, where the water level is just below the rim, a concave surface forms. This means the water level at the edges of the glass is slightly higher than the level at the center. In this glass, the cork always floats at the edge since the water level is highest there.

In the second glass, where the water level is just above the rim of the glass, a convex surface forms because the water level at the center is higher than that at the edges. In this glass, the cork always floats at the center.

Dig a little deeper:

Why is the water level higher at the edges of one glass and in the center of the other? The reason has to do with how water molecules are attracted to each other and to the walls of the glass.

As you learned in "Soap-Powered Boat" on page 123, water molecules form a type of net through hydrogen bonds. They prefer to stick to something—either to each other, or to the walls of the glass. In the glass of water where the water level is just below the rim, the water molecules at the edges are attracted to the glass. The adhesive forces between the water molecules and the glass are greater than those between the liquid molecules. Therefore, as many water molecules as possible try to have contact with the glass, causing the water level at the edges to creep up slightly higher than in the middle of the glass. The concave surface that is formed is called a *meniscus*.

In the overfilled glass, the water molecules at the edges are not given the choice between sticking to each other or to the glass. Instead, they are forced to choose between sticking to each other or spilling out of the glass. Rather than spill, the water molecules hold on to each other as long as possible. They pile up at the center, and the water level there rises slightly, creating a convex surface.

No-Light Lava Lamp

In 1964, Craven Walker invented the Lava Lite, a lamp where colored blobs of wax float up and down. Here's how you can simulate a Lava Lite, using similar principles but without the light!

This is what you'll need:

½ cup water
A clear glass jar or drinking glass, big enough
    to hold about a cup of liquid
½ cup vegetable oil
⅓ cup water
4 or 5 tablespoons salt

Here's what to do:

1. Pour the water into the jar.
2. Add the vegetable oil and record what happens to the liquids inside the jar.
3. Slowly sprinkle the salt into the jar. Record what happens to the liquids inside the jar.

What you should notice:

◆ When you add the vegetable oil to the jar, the liquids may appear to mix at first, but after a little while the water will settle at the bottom and the oil will float on top.

◆ When you sprinkle the salt into the jar, clear blobs of oil fall to the bottom of the jar and then slowly float back up.

Here's what's happening:

When you pour the oil over the water, the oil floats on top because it is less dense than water. Density alone, however, does not account for the two distinct layers. Water and oil are *immiscible* liquids—they do not mix into solution. No mater how much you shake the jar, after a while, the oil and water layers will separate.

When you sprinkle the salt over the layer of oil, at first it may seem to float on top of the oil. But the grains of salt are heavy, and eventually they fall to the bottom of the jar. When they fall, they may take a blob of oil down too. You might notice that the oil blobs sitting at the bottom of the water layer have a grainy coating of salt. This salt coating is stuck to the oil blob and anchors it down.

Salt dissolves in water, though, and eventually the salt coating of the oil blob disappears. At that point, the oil blob is no longer weighted down, and floats back up to the top of the water layer.

Craven Walker's lamp works on the same principles, except it doesn't use things like salt, water, and oil. Instead, the "lava" in his lamp is a liquid whose density changes based on temperature. The light source in this kind of lamp is at the bottom, which means there is a lot of heat at the bottom. When the lava is at the top of the lamp, it is far from the heat source and cooler in temperature. Cool lava is denser than the liquid surrounding it, so it falls to the bottom of the lamp. There near the heat source, however, the lava gets warmer and expands to a greater volume. Since increasing volume decreases density (see "Cartesian Diver" on page 134 for more explanation), the warm lava is able to float to the top of the lamp. The heating and cooling cycles continue as long as the lamp is on.

Dig a little deeper:

Most materials are classified into two different categories in relationship to the way they mix with water: *hydrophobic* materials and *hydrophilic* materials. Hydrophobic substances are chemically unable to mix with water (the word *hydrophobic* actually means "water-fearing"). Hydrophilic (meaning "water-loving") substances, on the other hand, easily dissolve in water. In addition to the density difference, the reason that you will always see a distinct oil layer above the water layer is because of oil's hydrophobic nature.

Things to try:

→ Try replacing salt with other materials, like sugar, baking soda, or baby powder. Do your results differ?

Baking Soda Bubbles
Watch how ordinary soap bubbles float on a
bed of carbon dioxide.

This is what you'll need:

½ cup baking soda
1 cup vinegar
3 large, clear containers that are taller than
    they are deep (glass bowls will work, but tall
    glass vases are better)
Bubbles and a bubble wand

Here's what to do:

1. Pour half the baking soda into one container and half the vinegar into another.
2. Combine the remaining baking soda and remaining vinegar in the third container. Record what happens when they combine.
3. Blow some bubbles into each of the containers. Record where the bubbles settle.

What you should notice:

◆ The bubbles float to the bottom of the containers that have either baking soda or vinegar in them.
◆ In the container where you combined the baking soda and vinegar, the bubbles should float on an invisible layer of gas.

Here's what's happening:

When you blow bubbles, a good amount of the carbon dioxide you exhale gets trapped inside the bubble, and carbon dioxide is denser than air. In the containers that have either baking soda or vinegar in them, the bubbles float to the bottom because of the carbon dioxide content inside the bubbles.

When you combine the baking soda and vinegar, a chemical reaction that produces carbon dioxide gas as a by-product takes place. A layer of carbon dioxide is created inside the container at the bottom. Since the gas inside the bubble is a mixture of carbon dioxide and other gases, it is still less dense than the layer of pure carbon dioxide. This is why the bubbles float on top of the layer of carbon dioxide.

Liquid Rainbow
Capture a salt and water rainbow in a tube.

This is what you'll need:

Paper cups for mixing water, salt, and
food coloring
Water
Food coloring in a variety of colors
Salt (or sugar)
Duct tape
A clear tube, approximately a foot in length, with
a fairly small diameter (inexpensive clear vinyl
tubing from a home improvement store will
work very well for this experiment)
A funnel that will fit in your clear tube (this isn't
necessary, but it will make pouring much easier)

Here's what to do:

1. Line up a different paper cup for each color of food coloring you have.
2. Add an equal amount of water to each cup.
3. Add a few drops of food coloring to each cup.
4. Now you need to add the salt, but you will be adding a different amount of salt to each cup. Write down how much salt is added to each color of water to keep track.
5. Add no salt to the first cup.
6. Add 2 tablespoons of salt to the second cup. Stir with a spoon.
7. Add 4 tablespoons of salt to the third cup. Stir with a spoon.
8. To each successive cup, add 2 tablespoons more salt than the previous cup, and stir it with a spoon.
9. Use the duct tape to seal off one end of your tube.
10. Check your notes to see which colored solution has the most salt in it. Use the funnel to pour some of that solution into the tube so that about 1 inch of color is visible.
11. Next, pour about 1 inch of the colored solution that has the second greatest amount of salt in it.
12. Continue pouring the different-colored solutions into the tube, being careful to pour them in descending order of salt content (the solution with the third greatest amount of salt is poured third, the solution with the fourth greatest amount of salt is poured fourth, etc.).
13. Record what the water in the tube looks like.

What you should notice:

◆ If you've poured the colored solutions in the proper order, the different colors of water will not mix.

Here's what's happening:

Each of the salt solutions has a different density—some are lighter than others, and the lighter solutions will float on top of the heavier solutions. Because of the density difference, a lighter solution tends to float on rather than mix with the solution under it (although, if you were to leave your liquid rainbow sitting long enough, all the colors would mix). If you are careful in this experiment and layer the salt solutions in the tube in order of density, you can create a rainbow of floating liquids.

Dig a little deeper:

Why don't the salt solutions blend into one color? Well, they will eventually. The solutions start to mix as soon as they come into contact with each other. The trick is to use a tube with a small diameter. It limits the amount of contact between two salt solutions. If you tried to do this experiment in a large bowl, the colors would blend much more quickly because the different solutions have a lot more contact with each other.

Things to try:

➜ Using a stopwatch, time how long it takes for the colors in the liquid rainbow to mix.

➜ What happens if you quickly invert the tube?

Cartesian Diver
Make this diver do your bidding!

This is what you'll need:

- A 2-liter plastic soda bottle with cap
- Water
- A ketchup packet from a fast-food restaurant

Here's what to do:

1. Remove the label from the soda bottle.
2. Fill the bottle completely with water.
3. Place the ketchup packet inside the filled bottle and screw the bottle cap on tight. The ketchup packet should float at the top of the bottle. (**Note:** *If, for some reason, your ketchup packet does not float, try other types of condiment packets. Soy sauce packets from Chinese restaurants, for example, are another good candidate.*)
4. Squeeze the bottle, observing what happens to the ketchup packet.
5. Stop squeezing the bottle, and observe what happens to the ketchup packet.

What you should notice:

- When you squeeze the bottle, the ketchup packet dives.
- When you release the pressure on the bottle, the ketchup packet returns to floating at the top of the bottle.

Here's what's happening:

This experiment demonstrates the relationship between buoyancy and density. *Buoyancy* refers to an object's ability to float in water. Something that floats is considered to be positively buoyant; something that sinks is negatively buoyant.

Buoyancy is also related to the amount of water an object displaces when it is immersed in a fluid. So long as an object weighs less than the weight of water it displaces, it will float. This is the reason that large ships are able to float on the ocean—they displace more water than they weigh.

Density is a measure of the how much mass an object has per unit of volume. Mathematically, density is:

$$\text{Density} = \frac{\text{Mass}}{\text{Volume}}$$

That means that if an object were to become compressed, its volume would be reduced. If its mass did not change, its density would increase. If an object were to expand, and therefore increase in volume, its density would increase.

The ketchup packet initially floats in the bottle of water because there is an air bubble inside the packet. This bubble is large enough to keep the packet floating when the bottle is not being squeezed. Overall, the ketchup packet is less dense than the water because of the air bubble, and therefore, it floats.

When you squeeze the bottle, however, you compress everything, including the air bubble inside the ketchup packet. The volume of the packet decreases, which results in an increase in its density. This forces it to sink. When you stop squeezing the bottle, the air bubble expands and the ketchup packet becomes less dense again.

Dig a little deeper:

Many ocean animals use the principle demonstrated by this experiment to control the depth at which they swim. Some fish, for example, have an organ called a swim bladder, which is able to be filled with air and can be controlled by the fish's muscles. To dive, the fish can contract the swim bladder and push the air out, making its body more dense. When the fish wants to swim farther up in the ocean, it can relax its muscles and let the swim bladder fill with air again. This makes its body less dense and allows it to rise.

Things to try:

➔ Temperature affects the buoyancy of the ketchup packet. Try this experiment again, using a packet that has been refrigerated for an hour and with a packet that has been left out in the sun for a few hours. Can you determine the relationship between temperature and buoyancy?

The Gravity-Defying Funnel Machine

According to the laws of gravity, things fall down. For example, if you set an object on a ramp, it will roll down from the top of the ramp to the bottom. In this experiment, you will make two funnels defy gravity by rolling up a ramp without being pushed.

This is what you'll need:

Enough books to make two stacks—one 1 inch high and
   one 3 inches high (you can use any type of book, but
   multiple copies of this one work really well!)
2 yardsticks
2 plastic funnels of equal size
Masking tape or duct tape
The cardboard tube from a roll of paper towels

Here's what to do:

1. Stack up the books into a 1-inch and a 3-inch stack.
2. Move the stacks far enough away from each other so that the yardsticks can lie across them to form a bridge.
3. Place both yardsticks across the stacks so that the two ends of the yardsticks are about 3 inches apart on the shorter stack of books and about 6 inches apart on the taller stack of books. The "yardstick bridge" should be V shaped. (See the illustration below.)

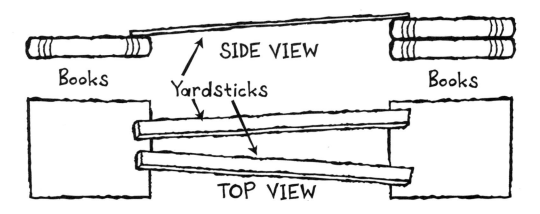

4. Tape the funnels together so that the bowls line up.

5. Place the cardboard tube at the bottom of the ramp and then the top of the ramp and record what happens.

6. Now place the joined funnels at the bottom of the ramp and then the top of the ramp and record what happens.

What you should notice:

◆ The cardboard tube rolls down the ramp when it is placed at the top and stays in place when it is at the bottom of the ramp.

◆ The joined funnels do the opposite—when placed at the bottom of the ramp, they roll up the incline. When placed at the top of the ramp, on the other hand, they don't move.

Here's what's happening:

Are the joined funnels defying the laws of gravity? It may look that way, but in reality, they are doing exactly as physics would predict.

The law of gravity says that an object's center of gravity will fall downward, from top to bottom. On the yardstick ramp, it seems that the "top" is 3 inches high and the "bottom" is 1 inch high. When you place the cardboard tube at the top of the ramp, it rolls down. Its center of gravity runs through the center of the tube, and rolling from top to bottom ensures that the center of gravity falls downward.

The joined funnels are shaped differently from the cardboard tube; they are narrower at the edges and thickest in the middle. It looks like the joined funnels roll "up" the ramp, but take a closer look at what happens to the center of gravity of the joined funnels, which runs through the two spouts. At the "bottom" of the ramp, the joined funnels are resting on the thickest parts of the funnels, keeping the center of gravity fairly high. At the "top," the joined funnels are resting on the narrow ends, which lowers the center of gravity. Therefore, even though it looks like the joined funnels are rolling up the ramp, you can see that the center of gravity is actually rolling down, just as gravity would dictate.

Things to try:

➜ What happens when you make the ramp steeper?

➜ What happens when you make the V wider or narrower?

Eggs-cellent Eggs-periments

Cooked or Uncooked?

These simple tests can tell you whether an egg is raw or cooked—without cracking the shell.

This is what you'll need:

- A raw egg
- A hard-boiled egg
- A marker
- A flat surface

Here's what to do:

1. Have someone else label the eggs A and B with the marker, making a note of which egg is raw and which is cooked.
2. Shake both eggs for 30 seconds, and then try to stand them up on their ends. Record which one stands up and which one cannot be balanced.
3. Lay the eggs side by side on a flat surface.
4. Spin both eggs at the same time.
5. Using a finger, stop the spinning eggs at the same time. Only hold on to them for a second; then let go.
6. Record whether one or both eggs stay still after you've let go.
7. Guess which one is hard-boiled and which one is raw.

What you should notice:

◆ The hard-boiled egg cannot be balanced on one end.
◆ After shaking, the raw egg can be balanced on one end.
◆ The hard-boiled egg stays still after you remove your finger.
◆ The raw egg begins to spin again after you remove your finger.

Here's what's happening:

Although the raw and cooked eggs look the same on the outside, their insides make them act differently in response to different forces. One factor is the egg's center of gravity—the area of an object on which gravity is expected to act. In an egg, the center of gravity is usually located in the yolk, because that is where most of the egg's mass is concentrated. In a hard-boiled egg, because the contents are solid, the center of gravity cannot be shifted. This is why the hard-boiled egg will never balance on its end. On the other hand, since the raw egg is liquid inside, its center of gravity is able to shift to allow it to balance. Shaking the raw egg for 30 seconds helps to "loosen things up" inside of it, allowing the contents to shift more freely.

When the eggs are spun, the contents of the eggs again play a role in how the eggs moved. In the case of the hard-boiled egg, the fact that the inside is solid means that it moves with the shell as one fixed object. In the raw egg, however, the liquid inside the egg moves independently of the outer shell. When the raw egg is spun, both the shell and the liquid inside the egg move. When you use your finger to stop the egg from spinning, you only stop the shell—the liquid inside the egg keeps moving. When you remove your finger, the egg starts to spin again.

Dig a little deeper:

The reason that the liquid inside the raw egg keeps moving even after the shell is stopped is inertia. *Inertia* is the tendency of an object that is in motion to stay in motion unless a force directly stops it. In this experiment, the spinning liquid inside the egg is not directly stopped, so it keeps moving even after the shell is stopped. Inertia is responsible for getting the raw egg spinning again.

Super Shells
How many phone books can be balanced on a couple of eggshells?

This is what you'll need:

- 4 raw eggs
- Scotch tape
- Scissors with thin, fine points (like cuticle scissors)
- 2 or 3 phone books, dictionaries, or other heavy books

Here's what to do:

1. Carefully crack the eggs at the small ends and empty out the egg inside, leaving the shell.
2. Rinse the shells with water and pat dry.
3. Wrap Scotch tape around the center of each eggshell.
4. Cut the eggshells through the tape to make four eggshell domes.
5. Arrange the eggshell domes into a rectangle on a flat surface with the cut sides down.
6. Balance one phonebook at a time on the eggshell domes. See how many phone books you can add to the stack before the eggs break.

What you should notice:

◆ The eggshell domes are able to support quite a bit of weight before they crack.

Here's what's happening:

Have you ever wondered how birds can sit on their eggs and not break them? The reason for this, as well as the reason that the eggshells in this experiment are able to support so much weight, lies in the shape of the egg. Architecturally speaking, eggs are eggs-cellent! The arch shape distributes any weight laid on top evenly across the entire arch structure. Dome-shaped eggshells can support a lot of weight because the load is supported by the whole shell instead of just one point on the shell.

Things to try:

→ See how much more weight can be supported with more eggshell domes.
→ What about cutting out parts of the top of the eggshell to illustrate the value of the keystone in an arch's construction?
→ What if the egg halves are put on their side?

Push an Egg into a Bottle

You can use the air around you to push an egg into a bottle, without even using your hands. Here's how. (You'll be working with fire, so it's a good idea to have an adult around.)

This is what you'll need:

A hard-boiled egg
A glass bottle whose mouth is slightly smaller than
    the width of the egg
Matches
Safety Warning: Be careful when handling lit matches.
Have an adult help you.

Here's what to do:

1. Peel the egg and place it on the mouth of the bottle. You need to make sure the egg won't just fall through the mouth of the bottle.
2. Take the egg away.
3. Have an adult light some matches, and immediately throw them into the bottle. They should stay lit in the bottle.
4. Put the egg back over the mouth of the bottle.
5. Watch what happens when the matches go out.

What you should notice:

◆ When the matches are lit inside the bottle and the egg is placed over the top, the egg may jump around a little bit.

◆ After the matches go out, the egg should slowly get "sucked" into the bottle.

Here's what's happening:

When you first place the egg on the mouth of the bottle, before you put the matches in, the air pressure inside the bottle is the same as the air pressure outside. There is nothing different about the air inside versus outside the bottle. But when you place the lit matches inside the bottle, they heat the air. Air expands as it is heated, and this makes the pressure inside the bottle greater than outside. This is why the egg may jump around a bit—the hot air actually pushes up on the egg. When the matches go out, the air inside the bottle cools and contracts. Since the egg is covering the mouth of the bottle, it acts as a seal. The contracting air causes another difference in the air pressure inside and outside the bottle. This time, the pressure outside is greater than the pressure inside. The air outside the bottle "pushes" the egg into the bottle because of this difference in air pressure.

Things to try:

→ Keep your fingers on the egg very lightly to try to feel how much the egg is being pushed.

Then Push the Egg Back Out
Use Bernoulli's principle to push the egg in the bottle back out.

This is what you'll need:

The glass bottle containing the egg from "Push an Egg
   into a Bottle" (see page 142)
Vegetable oil
Your breath

Here's what to do:

1. You may want to try this experiment outside, as the possibility of egg bits flying everywhere is significant.
2. Apply some vegetable oil to the mouth of the bottle, greasing it to make getting the egg out a little easier.
3. Turn the glass bottle with the egg inside upside down so the egg is again resting on the mouth of the bottle.
4. Tilt your head back and position the egg right over your mouth.
5. Blow hard on the egg. Observe what happens.

What you should notice:

◆ When you blow hard on the egg, it should slide out. Don't let it hit you in the face!

Here's what's happening:

When the egg had fallen into the bottle in the previous experiment, the air pressure difference that you had taken advantage of to get the egg into the bottle disappeared, since the pressure was equalized when the egg was out of the mouth of the bottle. When you flipped the bottle over in this experiment, the air pressure pushing on the egg from the inside of the bottle was equal to the air pressure on the outside.

However, blowing a blast of fast-moving air on the egg changed the balance of the air pressure. Instead of the fast-moving air pushing the egg farther into the bottle, the egg begins to be pushed out. This happens because fast-moving air exerts less pressure than still air. There is now a greater push on the egg from the air inside the bottle than the fast-moving air outside the bottle. The result is the egg sliding out.

Dig a little deeper:

This experiment demonstrates Bernoulli's principle, which states that as the speed of air is increased, the pressure it exerts decreases. Bernoulli's principle is used extensively when designing airplanes and other flying objects.

Invisible Eggshell
Make an eggshell disappear—with a little chemistry.

This is what you'll need:

- A tape measure
- A raw egg
- A glass jar or container that you can immerse the egg in
- Vinegar

Here's what to do:

1. Use the tape measure to determine the girth of the egg; record that number.
2. Carefully place the egg in the jar.
3. Pour enough vinegar into the jar to cover the egg.
4. Write down what happens to the egg when it is immersed in vinegar.
5. After two hours, remove the egg from the vinegar bath. Record what you notice about the shell.

What you should notice:

◆ When you immerse the egg in vinegar, there should be tiny bubbles floating off the eggshell.

◆ After two hours, the shell should be soft and rubbery.

Here's what's happening:

The bubbles you saw when you immersed the egg in the vinegar are by-products of the chemical reaction that is taking place. Eggshells contain a compound called *calcium carbonate*, which is what makes eggshells hard. Vinegar is really an *acetic acid*. When the eggshell comes into contact with the vinegar, a chemical reaction takes place between the calcium carbonate in the eggshells and the acetic acid in the vinegar. This reaction produces carbon dioxide gas, which causes the bubbles you see, and takes part of the calcium carbonate out of the eggshell, making it soft and rubbery. If you leave the egg in the vinegar long enough, the shell will completely dissolve, leaving only a thin membrane to separate the egg from the rest of the world.

Things to try:

→ After the eggshell has grown soft sitting in the vinegar, take it out and set it on the counter for a day. Does the shell get hard again? Believe it or not, it should! The remains of the eggshell react with the carbon dioxide in the air. This produces calcium carbonate once more—and makes the shell hard again.

The Incredible Inflatable (or Deflatable) Egg

Here's an easy way to make an egg "inflate," except that the egg will be taking in more water instead of air, and we're not going to be punching any holes in the egg. We'll just use the holes that are already there. To get the egg to deflate, we'll use the same process, adding one simple ingredient.

This is what you'll need:

2 eggs with "Invisible Eggshells" (see page 145)
A kitchen scale
2 glass jars or containers that you can
    immerse the eggs in
Water
½ cup salt

Here's what to do:

1. Weigh each Invisible Eggshell egg on the kitchen scale and record their weights.
2. Carefully place one Invisible Eggshell egg inside each jar.
3. Pour water into the jars.
4. Add the salt to one jar.
5. Observe the eggs over the next two days. Weigh the eggs once a day.

What you should notice:

◆ The more time the egg spends in the pure water, the larger and heavier it gets.
◆ The more time the egg spends in the salt water, the smaller and lighter it gets.

Here's what's happening:

How do the egg change in size? The answer is by osmosis. *Osmosis* is the process by which water flows from an area where there is a higher concentration of water to an area where there is a lower concentration of water. After the vinegar dissolves the calcium in the eggshell away, water can pass through the membrane. You are left with essentially two chambers of liquid—the liquid inside the egg, held in by the egg membrane, and the liquid outside, which is either pure water or salt water.

In the jar with the pure water, the concentration of water is higher outside the egg than inside the egg. In this case, osmosis causes water to flow into the egg. This also makes the egg "inflate"—the membrane now holds a higher volume of liquid than before. In the jar with the salt water, the concentration of water is lower outside the egg than inside the egg. In this case, osmosis causes water to flow out of the egg. This makes the egg "deflate"—the membrane now holds a lower volume of liquid than before.

Dig a little deeper:

The membrane around the egg is a semipermeable membrane—it doesn't allow everything through. Some things, like water, can flow freely back and forth, but the membrane is designed to keep things like proteins and other large molecules in or out.

Things to try:

➜ After you've watched the egg "inflate" in the pure water, take it out and place it in a jar of maple syrup. Maple syrup has a lower water concentration than the inside of an egg. Does the egg shrink? What happens to the consistency of the maple syrup? Does it get more runny?

➜ Place a vinegar-treated egg in oil. Does osmosis cause some water to come out of the egg? Can you see a water layer in the oil?

Float an Egg

Two seemingly identical jars of water—but in one, an egg sits at the bottom, whereas in the other, the egg floats to the top. What could make this happen?

This is what you'll need:

2 glass jars	Salt
2 raw eggs	A spoon
Water	

Here's what to do:

1. Fill the two jars with water, leaving some room for the eggs.
2. Place one egg in each jar. Record what happens.
3. In one jar, add salt 1 tablespoon at a time, stirring occasionally with a spoon. Record what happens after each tablespoon of salt.

What you should notice:

◆ When the eggs are placed in the jars of pure water, both will sink to the bottom.
◆ As you add salt to one jar of water, there will come a point when the egg floats.

Here's what's happening:

This experiment shows how a small thing like adding salt can make a dramatic change in how two materials interact. When an egg is placed in pure water, the egg sinks—it is much more dense than water, and so it is negatively buoyant.

As you add salt, however, which only mixes with the water, the density of the water increases. The density of the egg is unaffected by the addition of salt. At some point, the salt-water solution will become more dense than the egg, and the egg will begin to float.

Dig a little deeper:

Have you ever wondered why it is easier to float in the ocean than in a swimming pool? Well, the salt in the ocean does the same thing that the salt in this experiment does—the water is more dense because of the salt. That makes it easier for an object to float.

Things to try:

→ Use sugar instead of salt. Do you see the same results?
→ Use a hard-boiled egg instead of a raw egg. What differences do you notice?

THE GREAT E & M

This Battery Is a Lemon

Don't you hate it when you need a battery and you can't find one anywhere? This experiment will show you how to make your own battery—out of a lemon.

This is what you'll need:

- A lemon
- A penny
- A galvanized nail
- Alligator clips
- Copper wire (you can get this from any hardware store)
- A flashlight bulb

Here's what to do:

1. Roll the lemon on a table with some gentle pressure to mash up the inside of the lemon without breaking the peel.
2. Stick the penny and the nail into the lemon, making sure that they do not touch. You might need an adult to cut small slits in the lemon peel with a knife.
3. At this point, stick out your tongue and touch it to the penny and nail at the same time. Write down any sensation you feel.
4. With alligator clips, attach a piece of copper wire to the penny and another piece of copper wire to the nail.
5. Carefully touch both wires to a small flashlight bulb.

What you should notice:

◆ When you touch your tongue to the penny and the nail, you should feel a small tingle.
◆ When you touch the wires to the flashlight bulb, the bulb should light up.

Here's what's happening:

An electric current is created when electrons flow from one electrode to another through a conductor. In this experiment, the penny and the nail both act as electrodes. The copper wire connecting everything is a conductor. The lemon acts to finish the circuit while keeping the two electrodes apart (actually, the juice inside the lemon acts as the conducting fluid, known as the *electrolyte*). When you put this circuit together, you actually start a chemical reaction in which one of the electrodes loses electrons while the other one gains electrons. That makes the current, which lights up the bulb.

Dig a little deeper:

In a battery, since electrons flow from one electrode to the other, the two electrodes have to be different. One of them is called the *cathode* and the other is called the *anode*. The difference between the cathode and the anode is that the metal at the cathode gains electrons and the metal at the anode loses electrons. The chemical reactions that occur at each electrode are specialized as well; the reaction at the cathode is called a *reduction reaction*, whereas the reaction at the anode is called an *oxidation reaction*. In your lemon battery, the nail is the anode and the penny is the cathode.

The acid in the lemon juice plays a very important role in the success of the battery. The acid is able to react with active metals like the zinc in the galvanized nail. This reaction causes the zinc to give up electrons; this transfer of electrons is essential for creating electricity.

You may notice small bubbles near the place where the nail is pushed into the lemon. These are bubbles of hydrogen gas, which is produced when hydrogen ions in the lemon juice react with the electrons that are given up by the zinc.

Things to try:

→ Try using other fruits and vegetables like potatoes and oranges, which also have acids in them. Which will give you the strongest current?

→ Try other foods like hard-boiled eggs, bread, or green peppers. Do these work? Why or why not?

You're Electrifying!
Find out how and why you can be part of an electrical circuit.

This is what you'll need:

The lemon battery setup from "This Battery Is a Lemon"
  (see page 149), including the wiring to the lightbulb
A knife to cut through the lemon
Safety Warning: Have an adult help you cut the lemon.

Here's what to do:

1. While the wires are not connected to the bulb, use the knife to cut the lemon in half so that one half is left with the penny and the other half is left with the nail.
2. Leave each half face down on the table and connect the wires to the bulb. Write down what happens.
3. With the wires still touching the bulb, pick up the lemon halves and hold them in your hand. Write down what happens to the bulb now.

What you should notice:

◆ When the lemon is cut in half and the halves are not touching, the lightbulb will not light up. When you hold the lemon halves in your hand, the lightbulb should light up again.

Here's what's happening:

When the lemon is cut in half, the electrical circuit is interrupted and electricity cannot flow through to the lightbulb. But when you hold the lemon halves in your hand, the circuit is completed by your body!

Dig a little deeper:

In the first part of this experiment, when you touched your tongue to the wires in the lemon, the tingle you felt was from electricity being conducted through your tongue. The tissues of your body are able to conduct electricity; therefore, when your body completes the electrical circuit, electrons flow from one electrode to the other, passing through your body and lighting up the lightbulb on its way.

Some lie detectors actually measure the amount of electricity that a person's skin can conduct to determine whether he or she is telling the truth. Skin conductance can change when a person's state of mind changes, like when a lie is being told.

Magic Balloon

PART ONE: Divert the flow of water by waving a magic balloon.

This is what you'll need:

- A latex balloon, inflated
- A running faucet
- Someone with hair

Here's what to do:

1. Turn on the faucet—not too hard, but make sure the water is running harder than a trickle.
2. Rub the balloon on someone's hair. Rub it back and forth pretty fast. This motion transforms the ordinary balloon into a magic balloon.
3. Hold the magic balloon near the running water.

What you should notice:

◆ The stream of water bends toward the balloon.

PART TWO: Roll a soda can with the wave of a magic balloon.

This is what you'll need:

- An empty soda can
- A magic balloon (made the same way as in the previous experiment)

Here's what to do:

1. Place the empty soda can on its side on an uncarpeted floor.
2. Hold the magic balloon close to the soda can and record what happens.
3. Move the magic balloon back and forth and record what happens to the can when the balloon is moving.

What you should notice:

◆ The can will roll toward the magic balloon.

Here's what's happening:

Everything is made up of atoms; atoms are in turn made of smaller particles called neutrons, protons, and electrons. Neutrons are neutral particles; they carry no electrical charge. On the other hand, protons are positively charged particles, and electrons are negatively charged particles. Most objects in the world are electrically neutral, but you can upset the balance of charges in a variety of ways. One way is to rub two different objects together to transfer electrons between them.

When you rub the balloon on your hair, you help electrons move from your hair to the balloon. This gives the balloon a slight negative charge. (Incidentally, when charges get transferred, only electrons move—protons are fixed inside the nucleus of the atom. Electrons usually orbit around the nucleus, and are not as "attached" to the atom.) The more you rub, the more electrons move, and the larger a charge you build up.

When you hold the charged balloon near an uncharged object—in the first case, the stream of water—the electrons in the uncharged object move around. The electrons try to get as far away from the negatively charged balloon as they can, while the protons try to line up close to the charged balloon. After all, opposite charges attract, and like charges repel.

Because of the shifting of the charges within the stream of water, holding the magic balloon close to the stream bends the water in the direction of the balloon. In the same way, the charged balloon is able to cause the charges inside the metal of the soda can to move around, and then attract the can.

Dig a little deeper:

Most materials can be classified as *conductors* or *insulators*. The difference lies in the fact that electrons are free to move through conductors, whereas, in insulators, electrons are generally stuck in place.

Anytime two different insulators come into contact, electrons get transferred from one to another. Since electrons get stuck on insulators, a net electric charge can be built.

How can you tell which of the two insulators will gain electrons versus which one will lose electrons? Scientists have ranked different insulators in order of their ability to lose electrons. This ranking is known as the *triboelectric series*. Some common insulators are listed below:

your hand
glass
your hair
nylon
wool
fur
silk
paper
cotton
hard rubber

The higher on the list an insulator is, the more likely it is to give up electrons and become positively charged.

Things to try:

→ Test some of the insulators in the triboelectric series. Rub any two materials together and see what happens to a stream of water.

Make an Electromagnet

Explore the relationship between electricity and magnetism, and turn an ordinary nail into a powerful magnet.

This is what you'll need:

- Wire strippers
- 3 feet of insulated wire (make sure the insulation is fairly thin)
- A nail
- A 6-volt battery
- Paper clips
- A bar magnet

Here's what to do:

1. Use the wirer strippers to expose about ½ inch of metal on both ends of the insulated wire.
2. Coil the wire around and around the length of the nail, leaving about 6 inches hanging off each end of the nail. (See the illustration below.)

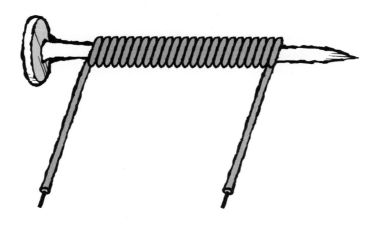

3. Carefully attach the exposed wire to the terminals of the battery. Now you've built an electromagnet.
4. Try to use your electromagnet to pick up paper clips. How many can you pick up at once?
5. Hold the point of the nail close to the north pole of the bar magnet. Observe whether it is attracted or repelled. Hold the point close to the south pole as well.

What you should notice:

◆ When the electromagnet is assembled and connected to the battery, it is able to pick up many paper clips at one time.
◆ There will be a clear north and south pole to the electromagnet, just as there would be to a bar magnet.

Here's what's happening:

Once again, this experiment takes advantage of the relationship between electricity and magnetism. In this case, the flow of electrons through the wire creates electricity, which then induces a magnetic field. Coiling the wire around the nail concentrates the magnetic field in one area. The metal of the nail already contains weakly magnetic particles; before the current is applied, the magnetic particles are arranged randomly, and there is a very weak net magnetic field. When the current is turned on, the magnetic particles are aligned, and a fairly strong magnet is produced. If you disconnect the wires from the battery, however, the nail loses its magnetic ability—the electricity is necessary to produce the magnetic field.

Things to try:

→ Reassemble the electromagnet with 6 coils of the wire around the nail. See how many paper clips you can pick up at once. Now compare how many paper clips can be picked up when the electromagnet has 12 coils, 18 coils, and 24 coils. Can you pick up more paper clips when the number of coils is increased? What does this suggest about the relationship between the strength of the magnetic field and the number of coils?
→ Assemble your electromagnet around a wooden dowel instead of a nail. Are you still able to see weak magnetic ability?

Eddy Currents

When a magnet falls through a tube, the magnetic properties
of the tube affects the speed at which it plummets.

This is what you'll need:

- A 3-foot length of copper pipe
- A 3-foot length of PVC pipe
- A neodymium magnet (you need this type of strong
    magnet to see a dramatic effect in the experiment;
    available at science supply stores)
- A pencil
- A stopwatch

Here's what to do:

1. Make sure the copper and PVC pipes have a larger diameter than the magnet or the pencil.
2. Hold the copper pipe vertically. Drop the magnet through the pipe and use the stopwatch to time how long it takes to fall to the bottom. Record the time.
3. Repeat the process using the copper pipe and the pencil, the PVC pipe and the magnet, and the PVC pipe and the pencil. Use the stopwatch to time each object. Record the times.

What you should notice:

◆ The magnet falls more slowly through the copper pipe than through the PVC pipe.
◆ The magnet falls more slowly through the copper pipe than the pencil.
◆ The magnet and pencil both take the same amount of time to fall through the PVC pipe.

Here's what's happening:

When the pencil falls through either of the pipes, or the magnet falls through the PVC pipe, the only force that is acting on the falling object is gravity. (There is friction as well, from the objects touching the sides of the pipes, but for the purposes of this experiment, the effect of friction can be ignored.) Therefore, the amount of time it takes for the pencil to fall through the pipes equals the amount of time it takes for the magnet to fall through the PVC pipe.

When the magnet falls through the copper pipe, an additional force is acting on the magnet—a magnetic force. The copper is weakly attracted to the magnet, and you may assume that it is the magnetic attraction that slows down the falling of the magnet. This is an oversimplified explanation—in reality, the magnet falls more slowly through the copper pipe because of the way the motion of the magnet affects the electrons in the copper pipe.

The magnet is surrounded by a magnetic field. The action of falling makes the magnetic field move, and the motion of the magnetic field in relation to a conductor (in this case, the copper of the pipe) creates electrical currents known as *eddy currents*. These eddy currents affect the motion of the magnet by producing a magnetic field, which acts in the opposite direction as the original magnet. The opposing fields are attracted to each other, and though the force of gravity is stronger than the magnetic attraction, the induced magnetic field is able to interfere with the falling of the magnet through the metal pipe, slowing it down dramatically.

This experiment will only work if you use a weakly magnetic metal, like copper, brass, or aluminum. If you used an iron pipe, the attraction between the magnet and the metal would be so strong that the magnet would not fall!

Dig a little deeper:

This experiment actually demonstrates the principle of Lenz's law. This law states that when a magnet is in motion, the magnetic field around it moves as well. When a conductor is nearby, the motion of the magnetic field induces a current in the conductor, which, incidentally, can be harnessed to power other things like lightbulbs (see "Hydroelectric Generator" on page 170). The current produced travels in eddies, or whirlpools, around the conductor.

The important principles that this experiment demonstrates are that not only can magnetic fields induce electric currents, but electric currents can induce magnetic fields.

Things to try:

➜ Get another length of copper pipe with thicker sides. Compare how fast the magnet falls through the thicker copper pipes versus the thinner one.

Field Lines
Visualize magnetic fields around different objects.

This is what you'll need:

An empty tissue box (you can also use pieces of
    cardboard that you assemble yourself to
    give you a platform)
A bar magnet (a strong magnet, like a neodymium
    magnet, may be easier to work with)
A deck of cards (or some other nonmagnetic object
    to raise the level of your magnet if necessary)
White paper
Iron filings
An electromagnet (see "Make an Electromagnet" on page 155)
Copper wire
Tape
A 6-volt battery

Here's what to do:

1. Cut off the top of the tissue box.
2. Place the bar magnet on the deck of cards to elevate it, and then place the tissue box upside down over everything. (The goal here is to raise the magnet so that it is close to the bottom of the tissue box. The bottom of the box will be the platform on which you will visualize the field lines.)
3. Place a piece of white paper over the tissue box.
4. Sprinkle iron filings over the paper. Observe any patterns that appear. Record your observations.
5. Collect the iron filings and save them.
6. Next, replace the bar magnet with the wire-covered nail from your electromagnet. Make sure it is not fully connected to the battery at this point. (You may have to cut a small window in the side of the tissue box to accommodate the wires from the electromagnet.)
7. Replace the tissue box and the white paper, then sprinkle iron filings on the paper while the electromagnet is not fully connected. Record what the iron filings look like at this point.
8. Connect all the wires of the electromagnet to the battery. Record what happens to the iron filings when the electromagnet is turned on.
9. Collect the iron filings and save them.
10. Finally, balance the tissue box on one end. Put the white paper on the top end and tape it in place. Poke a hole through the center of the white paper and the tissue box edge.

11. Thread the copper wire through the hole.

12. Sprinkle iron filings onto the paper. Record what the iron filings look like.

13. Connect the two ends of the copper wire to the leads of the 6-volt battery.

14. Record what happens to the iron filings when the wire is connected to the battery.

What you should notice:

◆ The field lines around the bar magnet and those around the electromagnet (when it is turned on) look similar: the iron filings will cluster around the poles and arc out from one pole to the other.

◆ The field lines around the conducting copper wire should look like concentric circles.

Here's what's happening:

Magnetic fields invisibly surround magnetic objects: permanent magnets, like the bar magnet you worked with, as well as objects that acquire magnetic properties because of flowing electricity, like the electromagnet. Even insulated wires conducting electricity are surrounded by magnetic fields.

In most magnets, field lines run from one pole to the other, with the field being strongest at the poles. In this experiment, you can tell where the field is relatively stronger by the density of iron filings in an area.

The field lines generated by the bar magnet and the electromagnet (when it is on) should look similar, since they are both roughly the same shape with a north pole on one end and a south pole on the other. The field lines around the conducting wire, however, look very different as the filings arrange themselves into concentric circles. The density of filings is greater closest to the wire and tapers off evenly around it.

Dig a little deeper:

Just from the arrangement of the magnetic filings, you cannot determine the direction of the magnetic field. You can, however, use the right-hand rule to make this determination.

Point your right thumb in the direction that the current is flowing through the wire (remember, current flows from the positive terminal of the battery, through the circuit, toward the negative terminal). Curl the other four fingers as if they were curling around the conducting wire. The direction that your fingers curl is the direction of the magnetic field.

Things to try:

→ Visualize the field lines of magnets in other shapes, like balls, disks, or horseshoes. How are they different?

→ Visualize the field lines in 3D by putting the iron filings in a small jar of baby oil and holding a magnet close to the jar.

Grape, Grape, Go Away
Show that a grape is repelled by both poles
of a magnet.

This is what you'll need:

- Scissors
- A drinking straw
- String
- 2 grapes
- A toothpick
- A heavy object like a large book or
        a bag of flour
- A neodymium magnet

Here's what to do:

1. Use the scissors to cut a small horizontal slit close to one end of the straw. Tie a piece of string to the straw and tuck it into the slit to keep it in place.
2. Push a grape onto each end of the toothpick. Tie the loose end of the string to the middle of the toothpick so it hangs freely in the air.
3. Position the heavy object on the edge of a counter and slip the free end of the straw under it. Make sure the toothpick and grapes are not touching anything.
4. Let the toothpick and grapes come to rest.
5. Bring one pole of the neodymium magnet close to one of the grapes (don't let it touch the grape). Observe what happens.
6. Let the toothpick and grapes come to rest once again, then bring the other pole of the magnet close to a grape. Observe what happens.

←—slit

What you should notice:

◆ The grapes swing away from either pole of the magnet.

Here's what's happening:

You are probably used to seeing objects be attracted to magnets (like paper clips or nails) or seem to be unaffected by magnets (like plastic). Objects that are repelled by magnets may seem a little strange—until you understand what is going on.

The explanation lies in how the atoms in a grape (actually, the atoms in water, since grapes are mostly water) are different from the atoms in materials that are attracted to magnets.

The electrons that are present in every atom are in constant motion. When electrons move, a magnetic field is created. You can actually think of each electron as a tiny magnet.

Materials, like iron, that are strongly attracted to magnets are referred to as *ferromagnetic*. In these materials, all the electrons in all the atoms will line up, resulting in very strong magnetization. Other materials that are weakly attracted to magnets, like aluminum, are referred to as *paramagnetic*. These electrons do not line up as well as in ferromagnetic materials, so the magnetization is weak.

Some materials, however, have equal numbers of electrons moving in either direction. The overall magnetic field is zero because the electrons cancel each other's effects. These materials are referred to as *diamagnetic*, and they are repelled by both poles of a magnet.

Water is a diamagnetic material. When you hold a magnet close to the grape in this experiment, the grape is repelled by the magnet.

Dig a little deeper:

Silver and gold are also diamagnetic. You can prove that they are by suspending a lightweight gold or silver locket on a string and then holding the neodymium magnet nearby. (Make sure the locket isn't too heavy or you won't be able to see an effect.) The locket should be repelled by both poles of the magnet as well.

Things to try:

→ Use other fruits like watermelons or oranges (cut into small pieces) in this experiment. Do you see the same result?

Volta's Pile

In 1800, Alessandro Volta showed that electricity could be generated through a chemical reaction. The voltaic pile was able to produce a steady stream of electricity in a very simple manner. This experiment is a simplified version of Volta's famous breakthrough that led to the creation of modern batteries.

This is what you'll need:

Scissors
Coffee filters
Lemon juice
10 pennies
10 nickels
Copper wire (you can get this from any
     hardware store)
Alligator clips
A flashlight bulb

Here's what to do:

1. Cut the coffee filters into small squares just a little bit bigger than a nickel.
2. Soak the filter paper squares in lemon juice.
3. Stack the coins and soaked filter paper squares like the illusration below.
4. Using alligator clips, attach one wire to the top coin and one wire to the bottom coin.
5. Carefully touch both wires to a small flashlight bulb.

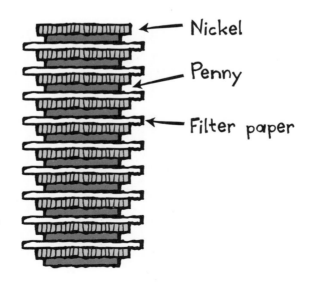

Nickel

Penny

Filter paper

What you should notice:

◆ When you touch the wires to the flashlight bulb, the lightbulb should light up.

Here's what's happening:

Just as you saw in "This Battery Is a Lemon" on page 149, electrons are flowing between electrodes in the voltaic pile. The electrodes in this case are the two different coins. The lemon juice is the electrolytic solution that conducts electrons.

The flow of electrons between the coins through the lemon juice creates a difference in electrical potential in the two types of metal. This difference is called *voltage*. When the circuit is completed with the conductive copper wire and lightbulb, electricity flows through the voltaic pile and lights the bulb. The more layers you have in your battery, the greater the difference in electrical potential between the top and the bottom of the pile, and the greater the voltage will be.

Dig a little deeper:

Originally, Volta did this experiment with zinc and silver disks and salt water as his electrolyte, and he was able to invent the world's first battery that could deliver a sustained electric charge.

Things to try:

→ Use different coins, like dimes and quarters. Does the bulb still light up?

→ Use alternating strips of aluminum foil and steel. Do you still produce electricity?

→ Using a voltmeter, compare the amount of electricity that is produced by different types of metals used in your voltaic pile.

→ What happens if you don't use an electrolyte? What happens if the electrolytic solution dries out?

Kelvin Water Dropper
Use falling water to create a high-voltage generator.

This is what you'll need:

Can opener
2 small tin cans (that hold around 10 ounces),
     empty and clean
2 large tin cans (that hold around 4 cups),
     empty and clean
Thick, insulating electrical tape
2 wire coat hangers, untwisted
2 large blocks of Styrofoam
A large bucket
Safety Warning: Have an adult help you with punching holes into the cans.

Here's what to do:

1. Using the can opener, remove the bottoms from the small cans.
2. Use electrical tape to attach the ends of the untwisted wire hanger to one small can and one large can. The small can will be suspended on the wire above the large one. Repeat this process with the other hanger and set of cans.
3. Arrange the cans so that a small can is above each large can, but the wires connecting the cans cross in the middle about ½ inch apart. Each small can should be positioned above the large can so that it is not connected to the wire. (See the illustration below.)

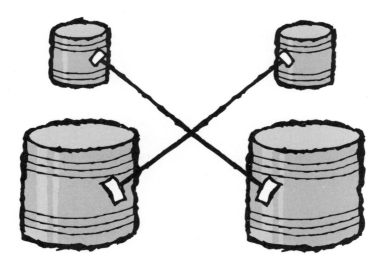

4. Place the large cans on the blocks of Styrofoam.

5. Have an adult help you punch two holes in the bottom of the bucket so that water will drip through the small cans into the larger ones. Position the bucket on a shelf above the height of the small cans. Make sure that the cans line up well with where the holes are; adjust them by bending the wire if necessary.

6. Fill the bucket with water. Observe what happens as the water drips down.

What you should notice:

◆ If the wires are close enough together, you should see sparks fly between them while the water drips down.

◆ Near the small cans, you may see small droplets of water flying sideways or even upward away from the cans.

Here's what's happening:

When any two different materials rub together, electrons tend to travel, which can also lead to a difference in charge. Even water molecules can become charged by rubbing against molecules in the air—that little bit of interaction is enough to cause electrons to transfer. In addition, there are all sorts of charged particles in water, such as dissolved salts and other impurities. However, at first the water flowing out of the holes in the bucket will be uncharged.

At some point, one of the streams of water coming out of one of the holes will become slightly charged—an extra electron will be transferred or a salt molecule will fall through one of the streams. Say a droplet of water that is positively charged falls out of the hole on the right and hits the large can on the right. This slight positive charge will drive the large can to become positively charged as well. Since the large can on the right is connected to the small can on the left, it too will become positively charged. The positive charge in the small can on the left will attract negatively charged particles into the stream of water flowing through it.

Once the process starts, more and more charge builds up in the cans. Any positive ions in the water will be attracted to one stream, whereas the negative ions will be attracted to the other stream. In fact, the stronger the charge on one side gets, the more it tends to force the other side to take on an opposite electric charge.

At some point, the charge difference between the wires becomes so great that a spark jumps between them. The spark removes the charge difference, resetting the system. As long as water flows through the bucket, a charge difference will spontaneously build up again and again.

Dig a little deeper:

A few droplets of water may be observed defying gravity and flying upward. This is also caused by electrostatic repulsion. Every so often, a water drop of the "wrong" charge will come near a can. For example, a negatively charged water drop may accidentally end up near the negatively charged can. Since like charges repel, the drop is driven away from the can.

Things to try:

→ See if the voltage generated by the water dropper is enough to light a small lightbulb by using extra wire to connect the bulb to the cans.

Great Electroplating

Move metal one atom at a time to create a
sparkly piece of art.

This is what you'll need:

Vinegar
A plastic container
An iron nail or brass key, cleaned with dish soap
4 tablespoons salt
A strip of copper (available at hardware stores)
Insulated copper wire
Wire strippers
A 6-volt battery

Here's what to do:

1. Pour enough vinegar into the container to submerge the nail or key. Add the salt and mix to dissolve.
2. Bend an edge of the copper strip so that it hangs over the edge of the container.
3. Cut two pieces of wire, each about a foot in length. Strip both ends of each wire.
4. Wrap one end of one of the wires around the copper strip. Wrap the other end around the positive terminal of the 6-volt battery.
5. Wrap one end of the second wire around the nail or key. Wrap the other end around the negative terminal of the battery.
6. Hang both the copper strip and the other object inside the plastic container, making sure that both objects are partially submerged, that the wires don't cross, and that the two objects do not touch.
7. Observe what happens to the objects over the next hour.

What you should notice:

◆ After 15 to 20 minutes, the nail or the key should start to look coppery.
◆ The object should be fully copperplated at the end of an hour.
◆ The copper strip changes over time as well; when it is removed from the vinegar–salt bath after an hour, it feels brittle.

Here's what's happening:

When the electric current passes through the electroplating setup, one metal loses electrons while the other metal gains electrons. The two different metals you use in this experiment have different tendencies toward losing electrons. In this case, copper is more likely to lose electrons than either iron or brass; therefore, copper is considered the more active of the metals. The more active metal of the two is the anode and the less active metal is the cathode.

Merely losing and gaining electrons does not explain how a layer of metal is transferred during electroplating. When the copper strip loses electrons, copper ions are formed in a process called *ionization*. These copper ions are dissolved into the electrolyte (in this case, the vinegar-salt bath). At the cathode (the nail or the key), positively charged metal ions can gain electrons. The metal in the nail or key is not getting ionized, so the only metal ions available to gain electrons are the copper ions in the electrolytic bath. When the copper ions gain electrons, they once again become copper atoms; since the process occurs at the cathode, the copper atoms are deposited there. Over time, a layer of copper will plate the cathode.

The reason that the copper strip feels more brittle after the electroplating is complete is because this process literally takes copper out of the anode and deposits it on the cathode. The longer you continue the process of copperplating, the more the copper strip would have dissolved.

Dig a little deeper:

Electroplating is used every day in a variety of ways. Cheap jewelry is gold plated to make it look more valuable. Silver plating is used on forks and spoons to make them look more sophisticated. Steel car parts are electroplated with nickel to provide protection from corrosion and then covered with a layer of chrome to keep them looking shiny.

Things to try:

→ Replace the copper strip with a nickel strip (or a nickel taped in place), but leave the copperplated key. Turn the setup on again, and see what happens. Since nickel is a more active metal than copper, do you get another layer on the key?

Hydroelectric Generator
Use your faucet to generate electricity.

This is what you'll need:

A shoe box
A 6-millimeter–diameter wooden dowel, 2 feet long
Measuring tape
A marker
Cardboard
4 disk-shaped neodymium magnets
Glue
About 100 yards of 24-gauge insulated copper wire
A cork
Electrical tape
Modeling clay
Plastic spoons
A small lightbulb

Here's what to do:

1. Poke a hole in each end of the shoe box large enough for the dowel to fit through about ½ inch down from the rim of the shoe box. Position the holes so the dowel runs lengthwise through the box.
2. Measure the distance between the dowel and the bottom of the shoe box. Use this information to draw two circles on the cardboard using the measurement as the radius (the goal here is to have a circle that can easily rotate inside the shoe box with the dowel as its axis). Cut the cardboard circles out.
3. Poke holes through the circles that are large enough for the dowel to fit through. Make the hole in one circle slightly larger. This circle will not rotate, and you do not want it to hinder the rotation of the dowel. Mark the circle with the larger hole "Stator." Mark the other circle "Rotor."
4. Determine which sides of the magnets correspond to the north poles (if they are not marked, you can use a magnetic compass to determine the north pole of the disk magnet).
5. Put a drop of glue on the north poles of two of the magnets. Put a drop of glue on the south poles of the other two magnets. Glue them to the Rotor so that the top-facing side alternates in polarity (N-S-N-S) as you go around the circle.

6. Loosely wrap the copper wire around the cork, leaving about a foot hanging off one end. You need to go around about 200 times, so keep winding!

7. Carefully slip the coil off the cork. Secure it with one or two small pieces of electrical tape.

8. Leaving about 4 inches loose, make another 200-turn coil, securing it with electrical tape as well.

9. Repeat this process until you have four coils, with about 4 inches of wire in between the coils and at least a foot hanging off both ends.

10. Tape the coils to the Stator circle, making sure that the coils alternate between winding clockwise and counterclockwise. Follow the arrows in the illustration below to make sure the coils are arranged properly.

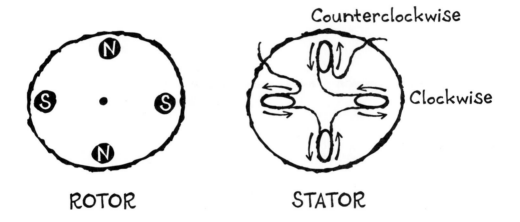

11. Push the dowel through one of the holes in the shoe box and then slide the Rotor and the Stator on the dowel, making sure the magnets and the coils face each other.

12. Push the dowel through the other hole in the box. Leave a good length sticking out of the Stator side of the box.

13. Glue the Stator to the side of the box, making sure the dowel can still rotate.

14. Mold a bit of modeling clay to the dowel between the Rotor and the Stator so that the two circles are about ½ inch apart. Twirl the dowel, making sure the Rotor can rotate. Mold a bit of modeling clay behind the Rotor as well, to make sure it doesn't slide back.

15. Mold a lump of modeling clay at the end of the dowel hanging out of the Stator end of the box.

16. Cut the handles off 8 to 10 plastic spoons.

17. Push the spoon heads into the modeling clay, making sure they are all facing the same way. This will be the turbine. (See the illustration below.)

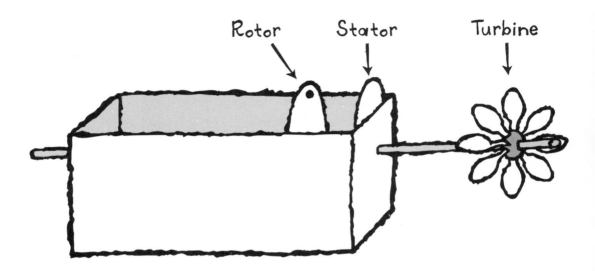

Rotor   Stator   Turbine

18. Connect the wires hanging off the Stator to a small lightbulb using electrical tape.
19. Position the shoe box on the edge of a sink so that the turbine is under the faucet.
20. Turn the water on so that the falling stream turns the turbine. Observe what happens to the light.

Optional: If you have a voltmeter, use it to measure how much electricity your hydroelectric generator is producing.

What you should notice:

◆ When the turbine spins, the lightbulb should light up.

Here's what's happening:

Just as you've seen before, when a moving magnetic field comes close to a conductor (in this case, the coils of copper wire), a current is generated in accordance with Lenz's law. In your hydroelectric generator, the flow of the water on the spoon-turbine spins the Rotor disk, which has the magnets on it. This creates a moving magnetic field.

The Stator disk, which is outfitted with conducting wire, stays motionless. But the moving magnetic field causes the electrons in the copper wire to begin moving. This motion creates electricity.

When the circuit is completed by the lightbulb or a voltmeter, the electrons are free to flow through the circuit. The electricity generated can be measured by the voltmeter or can be used to turn on the lightbulb.

Dig a little deeper:

In most electrical generators, powerful magnets rotate in close proximity to coils of insulated wire. The more coils there are, the more electrons are in motion within a small area. This generates more electricity than models with fewer coils.

Technically, the hydroelectric generator you have built is an *alternator*. In a circuit that uses a battery, electrons flow in only one direction through connecting wires. In your generator, the electrons move back and forth, or alternate in direction. The charge of the wire switches between positive and negative as the electrons change directions. This generator produces an alternating current, or AC, versus the direct current, or DC, produced by batteries.

CHEMICAL CONUNDRUMS

Fruit and Flower Chromatography
Is red always red?

This is what you'll need:

Filter paper, cut into 1-inch by 8-inch strips
A pencil
Some red fruit, like strawberries and raspberries
Some petals from red flowers, like roses, carnations, or tulips
A red marker
Red food coloring
Rubbing alcohol
Tall drinking glasses

Safety Warning: Be careful when handling chemicals like rubbing alcohol, since direct contact can be harmful.

Here's what to do:

1. Make sure you have enough filter paper strips for all the red samples you have.
2. Lay all the strips on a flat surface. Label them appropriately using a pencil. Make sure the label goes on the top edge of the paper.
3. Using the samples, make a mark on the filter paper, about 1 inch from the bottom. For the fruit samples, you can squeeze a drop or two of juice onto the filter paper. For the flower petals, you can place the petal on the paper and then apply pressure with a butter knife until some of the color has transferred to the paper. For the marker, draw a spot about ¼ inch in diameter. For the red food coloring, put one small drop on the paper.
4. Put about ½ inch of rubbing alcohol at the bottom of several tall drinking glasses. Prop the filter paper strips up in the glasses, making sure they do not touch each other and that the alcohol level is well below the samples. You may be able to fit two or three strips in each glass.
5. Examine the paper every 15 minutes, recording any changes in color you notice.
6. After 30 minutes, take the filter paper strips out of the rubbing alcohol and lay them flat to dry. Examine the different samples and compare what you see.

What you should notice:

◆ The samples will separate into different bands of color.

Here's what's happening:

The pigments that color the world around us, from flower petals to fruit to marker ink, are made from different chemical compounds. These compounds can be separated by size using a process called *chromatography*.

Chromatography was invented by a Russian scientist named M. S. Tswett in the early 1900s. It is used in a variety of ways every day, including being used in medicine to extract important chemicals from plants, in forensics to identify samples, and in sports to test athletes' blood for illegal steroids.

Chromatography is performed using all sorts of liquids, from water to acetone to strong acids and bases. In this experiment, you used rubbing alcohol because it is able to dissolve many of the chemical dyes in the samples you tested. The different parts of the chemical dyes traveled along the filter paper at different speeds because of their size, charge, or solubility. The result was several bands of color that appear at different levels on the filter paper.

Examine what chromatography revealed about what makes something appear red. What similarities do you see between samples? What differences do you notice? This experiment makes it clear that "red" in one material may be significantly different from "red" in another, from a chemical standpoint.

Dig a little deeper:

In many of the fruit and flower samples, you may have seen a yellow-green band and a blue-green band, in addition to other bands of color. These yellow-green and blue-green bands could be due to the pigments in chlorophyll. Keep in mind that all plant cells, even those that are not green in color, contain chlorophyll.

Things to try:

→ Repeat this experiment, replacing the rubbing alcohol with water or with acetone. Do the samples look different? Why would that be?

Chemical Copperplating

Give an iron nail a spiffy copper coat with a
special kind of bath.

This is what you'll need:

- 1 cup vinegar
- A glass bowl
- 1 tablespoon table salt
- Steel wool
- An iron nail
- 20 feet of tightly coiled copper wire

Here's what to do:

1. Pour the vinegar into the bowl.
2. Add the table salt to the vinegar and mix well to dissolve.
3. Scour the iron nail well with the steel wool to clean it. Rub it down until the nail is polished.
4. Place the nail into the vinegar-filled bowl.
5. Add the coiled copper wire.
6. Check for changes in the nail after one hour, two hours, eight hours (overnight), and after one day.

What you should notice:

◆ As time goes on, a thin layer of copper is deposited on the nail.
◆ The copper wire gets more brittle over time and may even dissolve quite a bit.
◆ If you touch the copper-covered nail, the coating will come off on your finger.

Here's what's happening:

This experiment demonstrates the principles of immersion plating. The nail is immersed in a solution of metal ions, and then a thin layer of metal is deposited over the nail. The vinegar–salt solution makes it easier for the metal atoms to transfer; in this setup, it acts as the electrolyte (the conducting fluid).

In "Great Electroplating" on page 168, you used an electric current to drive the transfer of electrons between different metals. In this experiment, you should see that an electrolytic solution can be enough to cause ionization, but there is a difference between the metal coatings at the end of each experiment. When you electroplated the nail or the key, the coating stayed on very well when handled, but the immersion-plated coating comes off on your fingers. The reason for this is that the copper coating is merely deposited on the nail because of gravity, instead of being bonded to the nail like it was in the electroplating experiment. In fact, you may notice that the copper coating is primarily deposited on the top surface of the nail—unless the nail is turned, the underside will not be plated.

Just like in the electroplating experiment, the copper source (in this case, the copper wire) lost electrons and formed copper ions that dissolved in the electrolyte. When the copper ions reach the nail, they gain electrons again to form metallic copper, which deposits over the metal of the nail.

Things to try:

→ Try immersion plating with other metals from sources like coins, hinges, or pipes.

Making Rust
Must iron rust?

This is what you'll need:

Soap-free steel wool
3 paper cups
Vinegar
Tap water
Salt water (mix ½ cup water with
    2 tablespoons table salt)

Here's what to do:

1. Rip or cut the steel wool into three pieces. Place each piece in a paper cup.
2. Fill one cup with enough vinegar to submerge the steel wool. Fill the next cup with enough tap water to submerge the steel wool. Fill the last cup with enough salt water to submerge the steel wool.
3. Examine the steel wool pieces in 15 minutes. Record any changes you observe.
4. Examine the steel wool pieces after two hours have passed. Record any changes.
5. Examine the steel wool pieces once a day for three days. Record any changes.

What you should notice:

◆ Over time, a brown coating of rust forms on all the pieces of steel wool.
◆ The steel wool that was submerged in vinegar shows signs of rusting almost immediately.
◆ The steel wool that was submerged in salt water shows signs of rusting within two hours.
◆ The steel wool that was submerged in tap water shows signs of rusting within three days.

Here's what's happening:

The steel wool you use in this experiment is made of iron. When iron reacts with the oxygen in the air, iron oxide forms. Iron oxide is commonly referred to as rust. The reaction is as follows:

$$4Fe + 3O_2 \longrightarrow 2Fe_2O_3$$

$$\text{Iron} + \text{Oxygen gas} \longrightarrow \text{Iron oxide}$$

For this reaction to take place, some of the iron metal has to become iron *ions* (electrically charged atoms that have chemically changed to gain or lose an electron) in a process known as *ionization*. Iron metal can slowly ionize in water, which is why wet iron rusts (the iron ions can react with oxygen dissolved in the water to form iron oxide). In salt solutions or acidic solutions, however, the ionization process is quicker.

The salt water in this experiment is, obviously, a salt solution. The presence of the salt speeds up the ionization of the iron enough to make rust visible within a few hours. The vinegar, however, is much better at ionizing the iron. Vinegar is acetic acid, and it can make iron oxide appear on the steel wool within minutes.

Dig a little deeper:

The chemical reaction that causes rust to appear on iron is a type of corrosion. It is the equivalent of the reaction that causes the green coating to appear on pennies. The difference is that when pennies corrode and copper oxide is formed, the copper oxide actually protects the metal underneath. Iron oxide, on the other hand, destroys the iron over time, making it brittle and useless.

In this experiment, you proved that salt water promotes rusting. This helps explain why the salt used on icy roads can be so damaging to cars if it is not properly washed off.

Things to try:

→ Compare the effects of other acidic liquids on the rusting of steel wool.

→ Can you dissolve the rust away using other acids?

Corny Invisible Ink
Make words magically appear.

This is what you'll need:

1 tablespoon cornstarch
1 cup water
Cotton swabs
Paper
A paintbrush
1 tablespoon over-the-counter iodine tincture
        diluted in 1 cup water
Safety Warning: Be careful when handling chemicals like iodine, since direct contact can be harmful.

Here's what to do:

1. Dissolve the cornstarch into the cup of water. Mix well.
2. Dip one end of a cotton swab into the cornstarch mixture. Use it to write a secret message on the paper.
3. Let the secret message dry on the paper.
4. Dip the paintbrush in the iodine solution. Paint over the entire piece of paper, and record what happens.

What you should notice:

◆ The secret message you wrote should appear in dark purple letters.

Here's what's happening:

Iodine is normally a dark red color, but in the presence of starch, it changes to a dark purple color. Foods like potatoes or rice contain a lot of starch. You can test this by adding a drop of iodine to them.

In this experiment, using the cornstarch solution to write a message gives the paper a source of starch that can be tested with iodine. The areas that are positive for starch become dark purple. This is how you can read your invisible secret message using simple chemistry!

Invisible Again
Turn your secret message invisible again.

This is what you'll need:

- The secret message from "Corny Invisible Ink" (see page 181) after iodine treatment
- ¼ cup saliva (to get saliva, just spit into a cup!)
- A clean paintbrush

Here's what to do:

1. Dip the paintbrush into the saliva. Paint over the letters in the secret message with the saliva.
2. Record any changes that you observe in the message.
3. If you do not see a change, repeat the experiment, using saliva from a different person, preferably a friend or neighbor.

What you should notice:

◆ Over time, the dark purple letters may fade and become invisible again.
◆ Some people's saliva has no effect on the purple letters.

Here's what's happening:

In your body, different proteins are responsible for breaking down different types of food. Many of these digestive proteins are found in saliva. The protein responsible for breaking down starch is called *amylase*, which is found in saliva as well as in the stomach and intestines. Amylase is an enzyme, which means it can be used over and over again to convert starch into a molecule that the body can use. Starches are broken down into sugars, which are simpler molecules.

When you add saliva to the secret message, any amylase in the saliva will convert the starch on the paper into sugar. When starch is no longer present, the dark purple color disappears, and the secret message is invisible again.

However, some people's saliva does not contain amylase. When saliva from these people is swabbed on the secret message, it is not able to convert starch into sugar, and their saliva will have no effect on the purple letters. Since the presence of amylase in saliva is genetically determined, it is possible that if your saliva does not have amylase, your parents' saliva may not either. That's why you should get a saliva sample from someone unrelated if it turns out that you don't have amylase in your saliva.

Crystal Stalactites

Grow a living cave in your kitchen.

This is what you'll need:

At least 3 drinking glasses
Water (the hotter the water, the better,
      but be careful!)
Table salt
Kitchen twine
2 metal washers

Here's what to do:

1. Arrange the three glasses in a row.
2. Fill the glasses on each end with hot water.
3. Add table salt to the glasses on the ends. Keep adding more salt until it doesn't dissolve anymore.
4. Cut the kitchen twine so it is long enough to hang into both end glasses and dip into the middle glass.
5. Tie one washer to each end of the twine.
6. Dip the twine in the salt solution. Make sure it is completely wet.
7. Place either end of the twine into the two glasses of salt water and lay the rest of the twine so that it dips into the third glass. (See the illustration below.)
8. Set the glasses aside for a few days. Record any changes once a day.

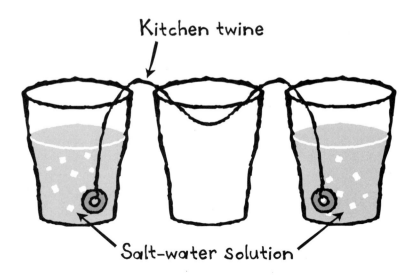

Kitchen twine

Salt-water solution

What you should notice:

◆ Over time, a stalactite of salt crystals will grow in the middle glass.

Here's what's happening:

Table salt is actually made of sodium chloride crystals. These crystals can be dissolved in water, but they will recrystallize when the water evaporates. In this experiment, the crystal stalactite you grow is the result of recrystallized salt.

How did the stalactite get into the middle glass? A phenomenon called *capillary action* is responsible. Capillary action describes the force that attracts liquids to solids. For example, when you put a drinking straw in a glass of water, you may notice that the water level inside the straw is higher than the water level of the glass. This happens because the material in the straw is attracted to the water and is actually able to draw it upward to fill the empty space inside the straw. Another example of capillary action happens in the capillaries of your circulatory system. These tiny blood vessels are able to transport blood partly because of the attraction of the vessels for the liquid blood. This helps keep the blood moving through your body.

The kitchen twine you used is not a tube, but it does have empty spaces between its fibers. Capillary action draws the salt solution into these spaces. At the spot that the twine dips into the middle glass, the force of gravity is a stronger force than the force of capillary action, so the liquid drips off the twine when a drop becomes too heavy. Sometimes the liquid drops hang for some time before dropping, and water evaporates from the salt solution. This leaves salt crystals behind. Over time, the crystals hanging from the twine grow until you see a hanging stalactite.

Dig a little deeper:

In nature, a stalactite is a downward-pointing deposit of minerals, usually calcium carbonate. When water runs through the cracks in a limestone cave, it dissolves the limestone into a calcium carbonate solution. As the solution drops from a cave wall or roof, some of the water evaporates, leaving a calcium carbonate crystal behind. This mineral is called calcite, and it can build up in size in the same way that your table salt stalactite did. In most caves, this process is ongoing, and the interior architecture of the cave will continue to change over time.

Things to try:

➔ Try other kitchen crystals, like sugar, baking soda, or borax. Describe the differences in the size and shape of the crystals.

➔ What happens if you fill one end glass with a salt solution and the other end glass with a sugar solution?

From Liquid to Solid
Some chemical reactions leave solid evidence behind.

This is what you'll need:

¼ cup water
4-ounce baby food jar
1 teaspoon Epsom salts
Plastic spoon for stirring
2 teaspoons ammonia

Safety Warning: Be careful when handling chemicals like Epsom salts and ammonia, since direct contact can be harmful.

Here's what to do:

1. Add the water to the baby food jar. Do not fill the jar more than two-thirds full.
2. Add the Epsom salts to the jar. Use the plastic spoon to stir until the Epsom salts have dissolved.
3. Pour the ammonia into the jar. *Do not stir.*
4. Let the solution stand for five minutes. Record any changes you notice in the solution.

What you should notice:

◆ As the ammonia mixes with the Epsom salt solution, a white solid settles to the bottom of the jar.

Here's what's happening:

Many of the chemical reactions covered in this book have included a clear physical change that confirmed that the reaction took place properly. In most cases, the physical change was either a change in color or the appearance of bubbles when a gas was created during the chemical reaction. In this experiment, there is no color change or gas produced, but there is a noticeable physical change—a white solid forms, which is called a *precipitate*. Precipitates do not dissolve in water, and can range in appearance from a faintly cloudy appearance in solution to large clumps of matter.

When Epsom salts react with ammonia, the following chemical reaction occurs between magnesium sulfate and ammonium hydroxide:

$$MgSO_4 \quad + \quad 2NH_4OH \quad \rightarrow \quad (NH_4O)_2SO_4 \quad + \quad Mg(OH)_2$$

Magnesium sulfate + Ammonium hydroxide ⟶ Ammonium sulfate + Magnesium hydroxide

Magnesium hydroxide is the precipitate, and it is made up of fairly small particles. You may have to wait anywhere from 15 minutes to a few hours to see all the magnesium hydroxide that this reaction produces settle to the bottom of the jar.

Dig a little deeper:

The starting materials, or *reactants*, in this chemical reaction are ionic compounds. This means each reactant is made of a positively charged and a negatively charged ion, and they are held together by the attraction of the electric charges. Magnesium sulfate is made up of a magnesium ion and a sulfate ion; when mixed with water, ammonia becomes ammonium hydroxide, which contains an ammonium ion and a hydroxide ion. When the reaction takes place, each reactant switched its ionic partner to create new compounds. This type of reaction is called a *double displacement reaction* because both reactants have partners displaced.

Moo Glue
Can you make glue from milk?

This is what you'll need:

1 cup nonfat milk
2 tablespoons vinegar
A saucepan
A spoon to stir with
A colander
Paper towels
1 tablespoon baking soda
Water
Paper
2 Popsicle sticks
Safety Warning: Have an adult supervise when using the stove.

Here's what to do:

1. Combine the milk and vinegar in the saucepan. Heat it slowly over low heat on the stove until clumps of white solids form. Since you'll be working on the stove, you should have an adult's help for this step.
2. Line the colander with paper towels.
3. Pour the heated milk and vinegar mixture into the paper-towel-lined colander. Let the liquid strain out and dry for 10 minutes.
4. Scrape the white solids back into the saucepan.
5. Add the baking soda to the saucepan and stir. Do not use heat in this step.
6. Add water to the saucepan one drop at a time, stirring frequently, until the mixture is the consistency of white glue.
7. Use your homemade moo glue to glue two pieces of paper together; glue the Popsicle sticks together. Let them dry overnight and then test how well your moo glue worked.

What you should notice:

◆ Mixing the milk and vinegar and heating the mixture causes the milk to curdle.
◆ Adding baking soda to the curdled milk makes it easier to dissolve in water.

Here's what's happening:

Whole milk is made from approximately 87 percent water, 4 percent fat, 4.8 percent carbohydrate, 3.5 percent protein, and 0.7 percent minerals. Nonfat milk is roughly the same except that it does not contain fat. The most abundant protein found in milk is something called *casein*.

In this experiment, the first few steps were designed to isolate the casein. Mixing milk with vinegar (acetic acid) precipitates the proteins in the milk—it makes them take on a solid form and stick together in large masses. The pH required for this precipitation is approximately 4.6, well in the acidic range.

When the nonfat milk separated into curds (the solid) and whey (the liquid), the curds contained all the proteins. Most of the other constituents of milk were removed when you filtered off the whey. Adding baking soda (sodium bicarbonate, a base) neutralized the curds and gave them a rubbery, sticky texture.

Dig a little deeper:

Since casein glue is so good at holding wood together, it was used in 18th century Switzerland in the construction of chalets. During World War I, casein glue was also used in the construction of wooden frame parts for aircraft. The main problem, though, was that casein glue absorbs moisture, which leads to fungal growths. This, in turn, weakens the binding of the glue. Nowadays, casein glues still have some useful applications.

SEE THE LIGHT

Simple Scope
Use a matchbox and a drop of water to magnify the world.

This is what you'll need:
- A rectangular matchbox with a sliding sleeve
- Scissors
- An envelope with a clear plastic window
- Tape
- A pencil
- Petroleum jelly
- Clean water
- Pond water
- Other things to view under your "microscope"

Here's what to do:
1. Empty the matchbox and take it apart. Make sure the sliding sleeve is open at both ends, so the matchbox tray can be slid completely through the sleeve.
2. Cut a window in the top or bottom panel of the matchbox sleeve. (See the illustration to the right.)
3. Remove the piece of clear plastic from the envelope. (Actually, you can use any piece of sturdy clear plastic, like from an overhead transparency or clear plastic packaging material. Just make sure that it's flat, that it's fairly strong, and that it doesn't distort images when you look through it.)

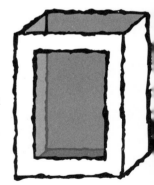

4. Tape the plastic to one of the ends of the matchbox sleeve. (Cut the plastic to size if you need to.) Try to keep the tape mostly on the edges of the sleeve so it doesn't get in the way of your viewing area.
5. Slide the matchbox tray into the sleeve, holding the plastic-covered end up.
6. Dip the tip of the pencil into some petroleum jelly. Draw a circle on the plastic with the jelly-covered pencil, being careful not to rip the plastic.
7. Place a drop of clean water inside the circle of petroleum jelly. This will be the makeshift "lens" of the microscope.

8. Place a drop of pond water onto the end of the matchbox tray directly under the water-drop lens. Look through the water-drop lens at the pond water, gently adjusting the matchbox sleeve up or down to focus. Record your observations. If the pond water is absorbed by the cardboard of the matchbox tray, remove the tray and coat the other end with a thin layer of petroleum jelly. Then replace the matchbox tray with the coated side under the lens, and add the pond water.

9. View other objects under the water-drop lens, like hair, onion skin, or small insects. Record your observations.

What you should notice:

◆ Objects viewed through your water-drop microscope will look quite a bit larger than they will to your naked eye.

Here's what's happening:

With this simple setup, you have duplicated all the principles used to make more complicated microscopes. The sliding matchbox tray is the *stage*. This is the part of a microscope the sample is put on, and it is adjusted up or down in order to focus the image. The water drop is acting as the *lens*. In this case, the lens is flat on one side and convex on the other.

Convex lenses magnify images. The thicker and more curved the water drop, the more magnification you will see.

Dig a little deeper:

Reading glasses, which magnify the text that the person is trying to read, are made from convex lenses as well. Can you think of other applications for convex lenses?

Convex   Concave

Vanishing Glass
The glass disappears like magic!

This is what you'll need:

A small object made from clear glass (Pyrex® stirring rods
work especially well; other things to try are glass
marbles, microscope slides, or small figurines)

A glass bowl or jar large enough to hold your glass
object (don't worry if the object can't be
completely submerged)

Water

Wesson® oil (regular, not light)

Here's what to do:

1. Place the glass object inside the large bowl.
2. Pour the water into the bowl, submerging the object as much as possible.
   Record how the object appears underwater.
3. Empty the water out of the bowl.
4. Pour the Wesson® oil into the bowl, submerging the object as much as
   possible. Record how the object appears submerged in oil.

What you should notice:

◆ Underwater, the glass objects may look a little distorted, but submerged in oil,
they partially or completely disappear.

Here's what's happening:

You have probably noticed before that objects underwater look a little distorted,
even though they do not change physically. The reason that they may look fuzzy or
disproportioned is because of the way light acts when it passes from water to air.

Beams of light have two options when they pass from air to another clear
material—they can be reflected, which means they are bounced back toward the
light source, or they can be refracted, which means they continue traveling
through the material, but they are bent a different angle than before. You can see
objects made of clear materials like glass because they reflect and refract light.

When a beam of light passes from one material through another, it changes
its speed. The difference in speed between materials determines how much
reflection and refraction will occur. The smaller the speed difference, the less

reflection and refraction, and vice versa. Every material has an index of refraction, which is a measurement that indicates how light slows down when it passes through the material.

The index of refraction of air is generally considered to be 1, which means that light does not change speed as it moves through air. When the index of refraction of a medium is greater than 1, the speed that light moves through that medium is slower than the light would travel through air. In water, the index of refraction is 1.33, which means when light travels from air to water, it slows down.

Wesson® oil and glass (especially Pyrex® glass) have very similar indices of refraction—approximately 1.47. Light passing through Wesson® oil and glass will experience minimal reflection and refraction because the indices of refraction are so similar.

Dig a little deeper:

Although Wesson® oil and glass have similiar indices of refraction, the glass objects will not completely disappear. This is because the shape of an object affects the way light bends as it passes through. In addition, any internal impurities in the glass will also change the index of refraction. With most glass objects you would use in this experiment, submersion in oil will result in a ghostly image.

Invisible Wool
Make wool seem to disappear.

This is what you'll need:

White wool yarn
A small metal washer
2 clear plastic drinking glasses
A large, shallow cardboard box
Rubber gloves
Methyl salicylate (available in science
    supply stores)
Safety Warning: Be careful when handling chemicals
like methyl salicylate, since direct contact can be harmful.
Have an adult supervise.

Here's what to do:

1. Wrap the yarn around the washer until the metal is completely hidden by wool. (See the illustration on the next page.) Leave about 10 inches of yarn hanging off one end to make it easy to move the washer.
2. Place both plastic glasses inside the cardboard box. (The box is there to contain any possible spills.)
3. With an adult's help and wearing the rubber gloves, pour about an inch of methyl salicylate into one of the plastic glasses.
4. Still wearing rubber gloves, hang the wool-covered washer into the methyl salicylate. Wait for the wool to become saturated with the chemical.
5. Carefully remove the wool-covered washer from the methyl salicylate and place it in the other plastic glass. Record its appearance.
6. Let the yarn dry, and record how its appearance changes.

What you should notice:

◆ When fully saturated with methyl salicylate, the wool yarn looks glassy and transparent. The metal washer will be visible through the yarn.
◆ As the methyl salicylate drains from the wool, the yarn becomes opaque once again.

Here's what's happening:

This experiment shows how the index of refraction of a material can be altered when it interacts with another material. In this case, saturating the wool yarn with the methyl salicylate gives the solid (wool yarn) the same index of refraction as the liquid (methyl salicylate). This makes the wool fibers seem to disappear.

As the methyl salicylate drains out of the wool yarn, the index of refraction of the wool changes back to its original value. As soon as the indices of refraction cease to match, the two materials are visually distinguishable.

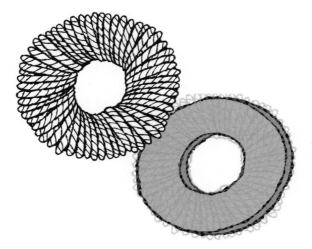

Powdered Milk Sunset

Have you ever wondered why the sky gets redder at sunset but looks blue the rest of the day?

This is what you'll need:

- A small aquarium
- Water
- A flashlight
- Powdered milk

Here's what to do:

1. Fill the aquarium with 4 to 5 inches of water.
2. Place the flashlight so the beam shines along the center of the aquarium.
3. Add the powdered milk to the water 1 teaspoon at a time, mixing well, until the water becomes cloudy and the beam of light is clearly visible through the aquarium.
4. Look at the beam of light from the opposite end of the aquarium from the flashlight. Record what color you see.
5. Look at the beam of light from the sides of the aquarium. Record what colors you see along the length of the tank.

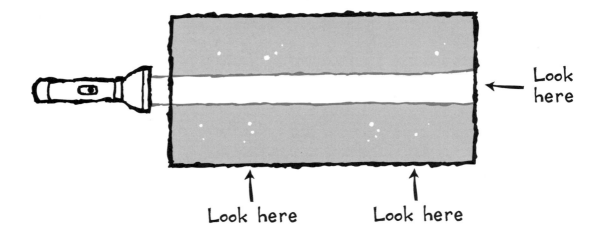

What you should notice:

◆ On the side of the tank near the flashlight, the beam of light looks slightly blue.

◆ From the opposite end of the tank, the beam of light looks orange–yellow.

Here's what's happening:

The white light that comes from the sun is made up of all the different colors. Since light is a wave, each color has its own *frequency* (how fast the wave oscillates in a given amount of time) and *wavelength* (how much distance is covered by one oscillation of the wave). When light travels through the atmosphere, some of the colored light is scattered and some of the light continues traveling. The scattered light gives the appearance of a color in the sky.

Depending on the frequency and wavelength of a particular color of light, it is scattered in different ways. The shorter the wavelength of the light, the more it is scattered by gas molecules in the atmosphere. Blue light has a shorter wavelength than red light, and it is scattered 10 times more than red light. When you look up at the sky during the day, when the sun is directly overhead and relatively close to you, the scattered blue light makes the sky look blue.

At sunset, the sun is much farther away from you, so the sunlight has to travel a greater distance to reach your eyes. The blue light waves are still scattered, as they are during the day, but because of the additional distance, they have scattered too much. The light that finally reaches your eyes looks reddish orange because you are seeing white light minus the blue light waves.

In this experiment, the powdered milk in the water represents the molecules in the atmosphere. The powdered milk scatters light from the flashlight in the same way that atmospheric molecules scatter sunlight. When you look through the side of the aquarium near the flashlight, you see a blue color because the blue light is being scattered. At the opposite end of the tank, the light appears reddish orange because all the blue light has been scattered out.

Dig a little deeper:

Since violet light has an even shorter wavelength than blue light, it is more scattered by the atmosphere. The sun, however, puts out a lot more blue light than violet light. Since there is so much more blue light than violet, the violet is "washed out" and the color we see in the sky is blue.

Things to try:

→ Repeat this experiment with a laser light. Do you still see scattering?

Absolutely Critical
How do you get total internal reflection?

This is what you'll need:

A small aquarium
Water
A piece of white posterboard larger than
    the top of the aquarium
Powdered milk
A laser pointer

Here's what to do:

1. Set up the aquarium on a table with a few inches of the bottom hanging off the edge of the table (you may need to access the bottom in this experiment).
2. Fill the aquarium with about 6 inches of water.
3. Cover the aquarium with the white posterboard.
4. Dim the room lights.
5. Shine the laser pointer through the water while adding powdered milk 1 teaspoon at a time, mixing well. Keep adding powdered milk until the laser beam is visible through the water.
6. Shine the laser beam upward through the water from the bottom of the aquarium.
7. Try placing the laser pointer in different positions along the side wall or bottom of the tank. Look for the position in which you can see a beam of light that bounces back into the water.

What you should notice:

◆ At many positions, you will see the laser beam bend back into the water as well as a beam of light hitting the white posterboard.
◆ At some positions, you will not be able to see a beam of light hitting the posterboard—there will only be a beam that is bent back into the water.

Here's what's happening:

When you shine the laser beam through the water, some light is refracted out of the water into the air (you can see it hitting the posterboard), and some light is reflected back into the water. You may have noticed that if shifting the laser source makes the refracted beam get brighter, the reflected beam gets dimmer and vice versa. This is because the total amount of light stays the same.

At certain positions, you will notice that all of the laser light is reflected back into the water. The angle at which the refracted beam disappears is called the *critical angle*. In the case of water and air, the critical angle is about 49°. When light traveling through water reaches the surface at an angle greater than 49°, it cannot escape the water and is reflected back. This phenomenon is called *total internal reflection*. At angles less than 49°, some of the light can be refracted out into the air.

Dig a little deeper:

The phenomenon of total internal reflection is very important in everyday life. Have you ever thought about how your telephone works? Information is transmitted along optical fibers. Light waves that are not parallel to the axis of the optical fibers hit the walls and get bent. Because the waves hit the walls at angles larger than the critical angle, they are totally reflected back into the fiber. This prevents the information from "leaking" out of the optical fibers.

Things to try:

➜ Repeat this experiment using other clear liquids like oil or light corn syrup. Can you find the critical angle in these liquids?

Benham's Disk
See the many colors of black and white.

This is what you'll need:

A photocopy of one of the templates below
Scissors
Glue
An old CD you do not want anymore
A black marker
A rotator (You can use a turntable, an electric screwdriver,
    or a hand drill. If these are not available, you could
    mount the completed Benham's disk on a toy top.)
Safety Warning: Have an adult help you if you use an
electric screwdriver or a hand drill.

Here's what to do:

1. Use a photocopier to copy one of the Benham's disk templates on the next page. You have to use the enlarging function on the photocopier to scale the template up to the size of the CD.
2. When the copy is the correct size, cut it out and glue it to the CD. If the black areas on the photocopy look gray or uneven, color them in with the black marker.
3. Poke a hole through the template to match the hole in the CD.
4. Place the CD on your rotator and turn it on at the lowest speed. If you are using a turntable, you can place the CD on the turntable, making sure the pin arm is restrained. If you are using an electric screwdriver or hand drill, secure the CD to the shaft using some modeling clay. If you are using a toy top, glue the CD to the upper side of the top. Try to do this experiment in sunlight or under bright incandescent light.
5. As the CD rotates, make a note of what colors appear. What color do you see closest to the center of the disk? What colors do you see in the next few bands outward from the center?
6. Have someone else watch the Benham's disk spin, and ask your friend what colors he or she sees. Are they different from the colors you see?

What you should notice:

◆ Colors appear as the disk spins.
◆ Different people may notice different colors or different intensities of colors.

Here's what's happening:

In the retina of your eye, which is the structure responsible for sensing light and color, there are two different types of cells: *rods* and *cones*. Rods help you see in low-light conditions, and cones help you see in bright light. Cones are also important for color vision.

There are three types of cones, and each is sensitive to a different color of light—red, green, or blue light. Each type of cone needs a different amount of time to respond to a color. In addition, the cones continue to respond to a color stimulus after it is gone, but they differ in the amount of time they do so.

People don't completely understand what happens when you look at the Benham's disk. One theory is that the black and white areas stimulate different parts of the retina. The white areas activate all three types of cones, while the black areas deactivate them all. In fact, you only see the color white when all three types of cones respond equally. The sequence of activation and deactivation while the disk is spinning happens so quickly that the nervous system gets "confused." The result is the illusion of bands of colors. The colors vary across the disk because the activation–deactivation sequence varies with the length of the black arcs.

When others look at the same Benham's disk, they may see different intensities of color than you do. This is because everyone's eyes are different in the way cones are distributed on the retina and in the sensitivity of their cones.

Dig a little deeper:

In 1894, a toy maker named C. E. Benham mounted black and white patterns on spinning tops and marketed them under the name "Artificial Spectrum Top." The effect, however, was first discovered by Gustav Fechner in 1838, which is why the colors seen in the Benham's disk are often referred to as Fechner's colors.

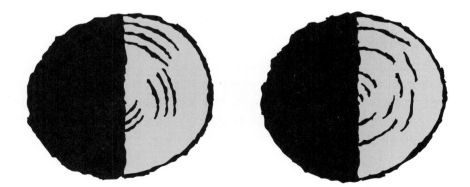

Benham's Disk templates

Fish in the Bowl

Is the fish really in the bowl, and what color is it?

This is what you'll need:

A black marker
Red, green, and blue construction paper
Scissors
Glue
4 sheets of white paper

Here's what to do:

1. Draw the outline of a fish on the pieces of red, green, and blue construction paper, and cut them out. Use the black marker to draw a black eye on each fish.
2. Glue each fish onto its own piece of white paper.
3. On the last sheet of white paper, draw a large fishbowl (large enough to fit one of your fish).
4. Lay one fish page and the fishbowl page next to each other on a tabletop.
5. Stare at the fish's eye for 20 to 30 seconds. Then quickly stare at the fishbowl. Record what you see.
6. Repeat the previous step for the other two colors of fish.

What you should notice:

◆ After staring at the red fish, you should see a blue-green fish in the fishbowl.
◆ After staring at the green fish, you should see a magenta fish in the fishbowl.
◆ After staring at the blue fish, you should see a yellow fish in the fishbowl.

Here's what's happening:

In "Benham's Disk" on page 198, you learned that special cells in the retina called cones are responsible for color vision. In this experiment, the fish image that you see on the white paper after staring at a colored fish results when some of your cones get tired. (By the way, the imaginary image is called an *afterimage*, because it appears after the real stimulus is removed.)

For example, when you stare at the red fish, the image falls on one part of the retina. The red-sensitive cones in that area get tired over time and stop responding to anything. When you turn to look at the white paper, the red-sensitive cones are too tired to respond anymore. Since our eyes only see white when all three types of cones respond equally, there is an imbalance and a color other than white is seen. The only cones in this situation that are responding are the blue and green cones—meaning the fish afterimage you see is blue-green. Similar things happen with the other-colored fish.

Things to try:

→ Use other colors of fish to see what afterimages you get.

Pinhole Camera

Use some cardboard tubes to make a "camera obscura."

This is what you'll need:

A marker
A cardboard tube from the center of a roll of paper towels
Scissors
Wax paper
Tape
Aluminum foil
A thumbtack

Here's what to do:

1. Use the marker to draw a line around the cardboard tube about 2 inches from one end.
2. Cut along the line with the scissors so you have a long piece and a short piece.
3. Cut a piece of wax paper slightly larger than the size of the tube's opening. Tape it into place on one end of the larger tube.
4. Cover one end of the short tube completely with aluminum foil and tape the foil in place.
5. Tape the smaller tube to the larger tube so that the wax paper is now in the middle of the tube, and the foil is on one end.
6. Use a thumbtack to poke a hole in the foil. (See the illustration to the right.)
7. Wrap a few layers of aluminum foil around the tube and tape it closed. Trim off any extra foil.
8. For the camera to work, you need a well-lit area. You'll probably have the best luck using it outside on a sunny day. Look through the open end of the tube and point the pinhole at the bottom of the tube toward something you want to see through the camera.

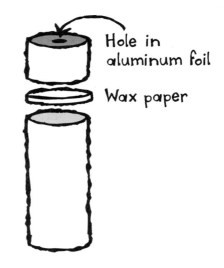

Hole in aluminum foil

Wax paper

9. Is there anything strange about the image you see in the tube?

Look through open end

What you should notice:

◆ The image inside the camera obscura should be upside down!

Here's what's happening:

If you held a piece of paper, like wax paper, next to a brightly colored flower, the image on the paper may reflect some color, but it really wouldn't look like anything. On the other hand, when the wax paper is inside the camera obscura, you see a complete image. The reason for this is that normally, so much light bounces off the flower to the paper that the end result is a jumble of overlapping light waves. The pinhole in the camera obscura lets in just a little bit of light—meaning that there is less overlap and interference, and it is possible to see an image inside the camera.

Why is the image upside down? This has to do with the way light gets into the camera obscura. Because the pinhole is so small, the image in the camera obscura is clear—light waves do not overlap and interfere with each other. The light waves can only, however, get into the camera in a certain way.

An object gives off light waves in every direction. When a light wave hits an opaque barrier, like the aluminum foil, it is reflected back. All the light waves that bounce against the aluminum foil do not get into the camera to make an image. The light waves that do get in have to be directed at the right angle to make it through the pinhole. As shown in the illustration on the next page, those waves go through the hole and then bounce off the wax paper. They way they travel, however, creates an upside-down image.

Dig a little deeper:

The principles behind the camera obscura were observed by Aristotle more than 2,000 years ago. He realized that you could see a picture of the sun projected onto the ground through the holes in a sieve. The first camera obscuras were actually large, dark rooms with a single hole to let in light used to view solar eclipses. People who used them noticed that they could see an upside-down image of the world outside the room during the day, but were amazed that the images disappeared at night.

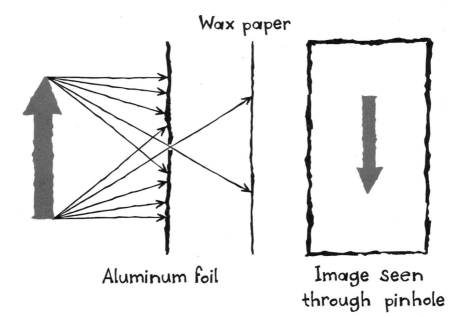

Wax paper

Aluminum foil

Image seen through pinhole

YOUR SCIENCE PROJECT REPORT

Your report for a science fair project will not be very different from the kind of report that professional scientists write when they conduct their experiments. Reports can vary slightly, but in general, there are 10 sections that should be included: (1) a title page, (2) a table of contents, (3) an abstract, (4) an introduction, (5) a materials section, (6) a procedures section, (7) a summary of results, (8) a discussion of conclusions, (9) suggestions for future or follow-up research, and (10) a bibliography.

Title Page

Check with your science fair coordinator for the rules concerning the title page. Some science fairs require your name and contact information to appear with your title, while others assign a contestant number in place of your name.

Table of Contents

The table of contents should be a comprehensive listing of all the sections of your science project report, including any figures, charts, or other data display items. Make sure there are page numbers in the table of contents, and that the pages of your report are numbered as well.

Abstract

The abstract is a short summary of your entire project. It is designed to let the reader of your report know very quickly what you did and why. The abstract should clearly state the question you tried to answer, your hypothesis or expected results, an outline of the procedures you followed, and a rundown of the actual results. It should not be longer than one or two paragraphs, so be clear and concise.

Introduction

In the introduction section of your report, include any and all relevant background information you uncovered during your research. This includes historical information about your topic and current uses and applications of your topic in the field of science you are exploring. Also, include a description of what about the project you found interesting and why you wanted to do it.

Materials

Use this section to give a detailed list of everything used for your project. Include specific amounts, weights, and volumes when appropriate. Also make note of any special materials that were used and where you obtained them.

Procedures

This section should be a comprehensive account of everything that was done during the experiment. Discuss which steps you were able to do alone and which ones required help from an adult. Try to include details like how much time you waited between steps, where you stopped to make observations, or which steps caused problems. The goal of the procedures section is to give the reader all the information he or she would need to repeat your experiment.

Summary of Results

List all of the results of your experiment, regardless of whether they support your hypothesis. Use photographs, figures, sketches, charts, and graphs whenever you can.

Discussion of Conclusions

In this section, you should analyze what your results mean for your hypothesis. Did you prove it to be true? Do your results contradict the hypothesis? Discuss any problems that arose during the experiment, and how they may have affected your results.

Future Research

If you can, outline some more ideas of questions that relate to your project and how you would go about answering them. If you had problems getting your experiment to work successfully, use this section to outline what you would do differently if you were to repeat the experiment in the future.

Bibliography

In this section, you should list all the sources you used to do your project and your report. Organize the bibliography into different sections, like books, magazine articles, Web sites, and encyclopedias. Unless you are creating a brand-new area of science, your report is not complete without a bibliography.

INDEX